Pray and Play
A Guide for Family Worship

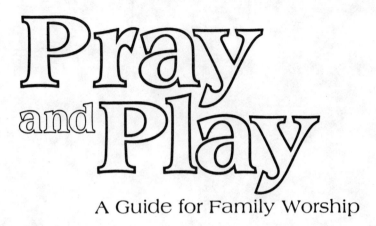

Pray and Play

A Guide for Family Worship

Donald S. and Nancy S. Whitehouse

BROADMAN PRESS
Nashville, Tennessee

Library of Congress Catalog Card Number: 78-050383
Dewey Decimal Classification: 249
Subject heading: FAMILY—RELIGIOUS LIFE
Printed in the United States of America

To
Ginny, Donna, Kenneth, and Ben
who taught us how to
worship as a family

Contents

1
Pray *and* Play?
Can the Two Go
Together?

Pray *and* play? Isn't it sacrilegious to mix praying with playing? Not where children are involved. Praying and playing are natural and normal elements of a child's world. There is no reason why the two activities shouldn't be woven together as an expression of praise. When Jesus said, "Suffer the little children to come unto me, and forbid them not: for of such is the kingdom of God" (Mark 10:14), he did not say that the children had to act like adults. Jesus accepted children just as they were. He did not demand that they behave or become like adults. Jesus indicated that adults could learn much from the uninhibited, trusting faith of children.

In our family the children have led us into beautiful experiences of worship. There was a time, however, when family worship seemed impossible. We tried to have daily planned worship with our children, then ages nine, five, and two, but too often the worship, though planned, did not occur.

A typical nonworship experience would take place in the following manner. Mom and Dad would summon all the children together to hear the Bible read and to pray. Inevitably two-year-old Kenny would sit for a second, then hop up and run around the room. Donna, age five, would attempt to tackle Kenny and force him back to his seat. Nine-year-old Ginny would become tickled at the ensuing chase, and Mom would struggle to maintain her composure. Dad would explode at such blasphemous activity and would loudly demand restoration of order. When, and if, decorum was restored, no one would be in the mood for listening. By that time Bible reading and prayer would be more of a ritual than a meaningful experience.

Obviously the strictly adult approach to family worship was not going to work in a family composed of preschoolers and a grade schooler. This approach was contributing more toward Dad "losing" his religion than it was toward enriching the spiritual life of the family.

Finally Mom and Dad decided to try various approaches to family worship. During the time of experimenting, the children made suggestions which were incorporated into the worship activities. The result was a "pray and play" format for a special weekly worship activity.

The special family worship was scheduled for Sunday night after returning home from church. The children put on their pajamas as soon as they got home. Putting on their pajamas at this time made them comfortable, and it eliminated much of the protest that often came at bedtime.

The worship activity began with the "breaking of bread." However, the "bread" may have been popcorn, potato chips, sandwiches, or any variety of picnic-type foods. This was one meal where the emphasis was upon "fun food." Conversation about the day's activities accompanied the meal. The two-year-old couldn't fully join in the conversation, but he obviously enjoyed the occasion. Eating and talking together strengthened the bond of family fellowship.

The next portion of the evening's schedule consisted of games. Action games were preferred for two reasons. (1) Kenny's eagerness to join in the fun soon rendered any sophisticated table game impossible to play. (2) Action games helped "work out the wiggles." They helped the children expend excessive energy.

Song time followed the games. For this activity, everyone went into one of the children's bedrooms and sat in a circle on the floor. The change of location helped establish the environment for a quieter activity. The songs were not planned in advance, but usually the first ones were motion songs. Kenny, the toddler, did not understand the words, but he did attempt to make the motions. Eventually these songs gave way to quieter favorites such as "Jesus Loves Me" and "Whisper a Prayer."

From this point on, if Kenny ran around the room or left the room, no one tried to make him sit down. Mom and Dad accepted the fact that he was too young to sit still for long. They discovered that if they did not reward him with attention, either in the form of discipline or laughter, he soon returned to the circle. He was given attention only when he was seated in the circle.

After singing a few songs, the children were ready to move into the devotional phase of worship. Dad would help Donna "read" a verse of Scripture by whispering the words into her ear while she held the open Bible. In this way she "read" aloud to the rest of the family. Then Dad would read a short devotional story. Following the story, the older children were asked questions about the content and meaning of the story. They always listened carefully to the story because they delighted in being able to answer the questions.

Next, the oldest child, assisted by Mom when necessary, read from her Bible. Then each member of the family took turns praying. Often Kenny would kneel beside someone, or he would hold his hands together and bow his head, just as he saw the others doing. His mumbling was unintelligible, but he was learning the practice of prayer.

This "pray and play" worship usually lasted for approximately one hour. No time limit was set for any portion. Movement was made from one part of the worship to another whenever it seemed appropriate.

As the children grew older and increased in number, Ben, the fourth child, took over the role of "disturber." Necessary and natural modifications were made to the initial "pray and play" format. The children became even more actively involved in planning, conducting, and participating in the family worship. Despite the modification, the principle of combining play and worship remained characteristic of the special family worship time. The appropriateness of this approach to family worship was validated by Kenny. As a preschooler, he wrecked many attempts to worship, but later as a first grader he eagerly would ask, "Can we have a worship service tonight?"

The pray and play approach is no substitute for brief periods of daily devotion, such as saying grace at meals, reading the Bible, or saying bedtime prayers. This approach is one way for a family to set aside an hour or more each week which can become the most enjoyable and rewarding time of the week—an hour of family worship.

2
Why *Family* Worship? Isn't Church Worship Enough?

Church worship experiences alone cannot meet the total spiritual needs of a family. Family worship experiences provide blessings which are not readily attained through other worship structures.

Strengthens Family Relationships

Family worship strengthens family relationships. No matter how old or how young the children may be in a family, that family will be drawn closer together through the experiences of home worship. This strengthened relationship will not be limited to parents feeling closer to the children or to the children having a greater understanding of their parents. Brothers and sisters will develop stronger ties with each other. Each family member will develop a more comprehensive perception and understanding of each other family member. Individual differences will be recognized and appreciated. In cases where the differences cannot be appreciated, at least a degree of tolerance and acceptance will be developed. And as individual family members develop respect for the God-given uniqueness of other family members, there will emerge a holy respect for and pride in their particular family unit. Just as they come to realize the uniqueness of individuals, they will come to recognize the God-given uniqueness of their own family. They will realize that there is no family in the world exactly like theirs, and they will realize their family has much to contribute to the spiritual welfare of other people.

One of the reasons that family worship strengthens family relationships is that the worship experiences open a new and deeper channel for communications. It would be difficult, though not impossible, to chart all of the channels of communications in a family. For example, much family communication takes place through the factual channel. "Where are my socks?" "Your socks are in your dresser." "I don't see them." "Well then, look on top of the washer. Maybe I haven't put them away yet." This channel of communication deals strictly with facts—what is and what isn't. Another channel, potentially emotional, is the opinion channel. "Don't you think white socks would look better than the red ones you are wearing?" "I don't care. I like these socks better than any others I have."

Despite the variety of family communication channels which could be described, most of these channels have two common characteristics: (1) Primarily, they are superficial in nature. Seldom do they reach deep levels of openness and honesty. (2) Also, the channels are defensive in nature. Much conversation consists of defending what one "knows" to be a fact or defending an opinion. Seldom in family conversations do we share or even admit doubts and genuine fears. (Often we do share superficial frustrations.) Seldom do we aggressively seek to express appreciation to other family members. We are so prone to be defensive that even when we make an effort to discover the real feelings of other family members, we shy away from probing too deeply for fear that they might reveal something we can't or don't want to handle. A father may shy away from any discussions of sex with his daughter. A mother may refrain from discussing death with her children.

Family worship provides a channel of communication which not only strengthens other channels, but it helps free up channels which become blocked. In one family the father and mother had had a bitter argument. The argument had not been resolved but had deteriorated to "grunt and groan" communication. At the time regularly set aside for family worship, the children began to ask, "Aren't we going to have our worship?" Both parents realized that though they did not feel like worshiping—certainly not with each other—they could not refuse the children. By the time the worship period had ended, so had the disagreement between the mother and the father. The worship experience had enabled them to reestablish meaningful communication.

Family worship creates a communication channel in which children learn to share hopes, feelings, and fears. Through singing and sharing Bible stories and life-situation stories which deal with the broad range of human experience, children can approach delicate subjects from an objective viewpoint and then can "hang" their own concerns on to the story structure. In this way the entire family engages in sharing concerns which often are so deeply embedded that they would never be verbalized through other than a worship communication channel. In a real sense, a holy avenue for communication is established—one seldom found in contemporary families.

The family worship experience creates a special environment which not only challenges children to raise questions and to express feelings but also makes them comfortable to state their own understandings and misunderstandings about scriptural and other spiritual matters. One family discovered that they needed to work on basic doctrinal teaching when their young son declared, "I love Jesus but I don't like God." The relaxed discussion which followed this declaration revealed that child had been equally impressed by the "wrath of God" stories in the Old Testament and the "love of Jesus" stories in the New Testament, but he did not understand how the two related.

Still another strengthening factor for family relationships is that family worship provides common experiences for the entire family. Many families do not experience a single common experience during a week, much less during a day. The greatest opportunity for a shared experience for all family members is at mealtime, but differing sleep, work, and school schedules eliminate breakfast and lunch as possible common experiences. The larger the family the more difficult it is to arrange a time or an event in which all family members can participate and can participate with a sense of joy and fulfillment. Age differ-

ences in children create differences in interest, which in turn
create a rebellion against experiences which appeal to others
of different ages. Even church activities often contribute more
to meeting individual needs than meeting family needs for
togetherness. Most church-related activities are graded for specific age groups which exclude family togetherness. The church
worship service might be one opportunity for a total family
experience, but preschoolers and younger children typically
find the church worship service to be too long and too restrictive to be an experience of joy and fulfillment. Even a church-
going family, however, may become so caught up in church
activities for all ages that they think they have common experiences (going to church) when actually they are a totally frag-
mented family. A home worship experience which calls for
and allows participation by each family member could be the
only common experience a family has on a regular basis.

One other reinforcement of family ties provided by family
worship is the establishment of meaningful family traditions.
Children love to repeat pleasant experiences, and from repetition will come traditions unique to each family. Traditions may
range from frequent experiences—like the tradition in one
family that the youngest member begins each prayer time followed in turn by the next oldest until the oldest family member
concludes—to such annual experiences as holiday or birthday
observances. In one family, the observance of Christmas begins
with all members gathered in the evening around a fireplace
with the roaring fire providing the only light in the room,
and the father opens a huge family Bible to read the Christmas
story from the Gospel of Luke. Observance of traditions which
stem from family worship cannot help but create strong and
lasting family relationships.

The experience of family worship, repeated regularly, will
create a communications foundation which will endure
throughout the changing phases of family life. The various activities which make up a worship experience can be modified
through the years to meet the growing interests and abilities

of the children in the family. Family worship can and should continue to be the one common family experience—the one communications channel—which responds to changes in the family situation but which improves rather than diminishes with age. Family members may outgrow the stories and activities suggested in this book, but they will never outgrow the blessings which come from family worship.

Family relationships are strengthened in so many ways through family worship, but there is one strengthening element which extends beyond the immediate family and the present time. Family worship provides a pattern (not a rigid mold) for children to model in their own familes. Because each child will have been an active participant in, and at times a leader of, family worship, he or she will know how to establish (continue) the tradition of family worship in the new home. Not only will the child-become-adult know how to conduct family worship, but the home worship experiences of the past should have been so meaningful that there will be no lack of desire to make family worship as normal and natural as any item of furniture. What better heritage could be passed from generation to generation?

Aids Individual Development

Family worship is important because it aids individual spiritual development. Through family worship, each participant, the adult as well as the child, will become increasingly aware of his self-value. The worship experiences will lead the participants through the awareness stage of their own sinfulness and need for repentance and forgiveness to the higher stage of realization that they were created in the image and love of God and that by his power they can be "more than conquerors" over the control and consequences of sin. They can "do all things" through Christ. Through the sharing and feedback, study, inspiration, and revelation that will come, the individual will come to accept his uniqueness, not with an air of haughtiness and superiority over others, but with a sense of awe—of

wonderment, of humility—and of responsibility to bring to fulfillment all the potential God created in him.

Family worship aids individual spiritual development by
teaching individuals how to worship. The creativity and sponta-
neity experienced will make each family member sensitive
to ways and times worship can take place in other settings—
even when alone. As the children take part in and plan for
group worship, they will have a growing appreciation and need
for personal worship as well as for different kinds of group
worship.

Moreover, family worship provides a means for putting faith
into practice. Because both the content and the methodology
of family worship is selected to meet the needs and expression
abilities of each family, each member will find that the faith
learned and shared during a structured time period will be
more easily expressed during unstructured time at home. And
the faith that one practices and shares naturally at home will
more likely be expressed naturally in other settings outside
the home. Home is the one place where each person should
feel comfortable in putting faith into practice, in expressing
personal convictions. Unfortunately this is not always the case,
even in so-called Christian homes. If faith cannot be practiced
at home, it is unlikely that it will be practiced elsewhere. Furthermore, attempts to demonstrate faith elsewhere will be
more hypocrisy than faith, and children are quick to perceive
hypocrisy.

Family worship aids individual spiritual development
through teaching family members how to use, interpret, and
apply the Bible. These same Bible skills are dealt with in Sunday
School and other church educational settings, but the value
of learning these skills in the home environment is that they
are learned in the individual's most used laboratory of life—
one's own home. What is learned at church is reinforced at
home, and vice versa. Learning Bible use begins with learning
the different books of the Bible and being able to locate specific
books, chapters, and verses. Learning to interpret the Bible

includes how to consult such Bible study aids as commentaries, maps, or Bible dictionaries. Scripture interpretation also involves seeking and following the guidance of the Holy Spirit in discerning the lesson to be learned in a given passage of Scripture. The guidance of the Holy Spirit is needed also in applying that lesson, that scriptural truth, to personal daily living.

Spiritual growth through family worship is not just an outcome for the children in a family. Both parents will be blessed immeasurably as they learn from their children. The simple yet profound questions children ask will push parents to new depths of understanding as they attempt to voice answers to those questions. The insights expressed by the children at times will astound the parents and make them even more aware of the image of God in every person—even children. Parents will learn anew the meaning of the Scripture phrases such as "a little child shall lead them" (Isa. 11:6) and "of such is the kingdom of God" (Mark 10:14).

Individual spiritual development will be aided through family worship by providing opportunities to deal with and prepare for life's crises. The major uncertainty about the crises of life is *when* they will be faced. Most certainly each person will encounter crushing experiences—some early in life, some later, some seemingly throughout their entire lifetime. The other major uncertainty about life's crises is *what?*—what will the crises be? Will it be death, lingering illness, or a physical handicap? Will it be divorce, desertion, or personal degradation? Will it be self-inflicted, imposed by others, or just an uncontrollable circumstance?

When we observe the innocence and sweetness of youth, we want to shield young children from some of the horrors of life. Yet in shielding them from the realities of life we may be doing them a great disservice. For one thing, children cannot be shielded from life's realities. Even if they have not gone through the trauma of their parents' divorce, they have friends whose parents have divorced. They need to deal with that reality, if for nothing more than to hear their own parents affirm their love for each other and assure the children they will not get a divorce. Children need to know that there is evil and wrongdoing and suffering in the world, but more important they need to know how God loves and cares for people even in the midst of life's crises. Children must be taught how God will help them in a crisis situation before that situation occurs. The family worship hours can provide an arena for anticipating those crises, and getting ready for them.

At least six ways family worship aids individual spiritual development have been identified. More could be added to the list, but they all could be summarized by stating that family worship deepens one's spiritual life. There is no experience which can equal that of a family praying together and for one another.

Follows Biblical Pattern for Family Life

The practice of family worship is in keeping with biblical patterns for family life. Consider these words from Moses: "And these words, which I command thee this day, shall be in thine heart: And thou shalt teach them diligently unto thy children, and shall talk of them when thou sittest in thine house, and when thou walkest by the way, and when thou liest down, and when thou risest up" (Deut. 6:6-7).

From the earliest days of the Israelite people, conversation and instruction about God were an integral part of family life. Discussion about God's commandments cannot be limited to a certain day of the week or time of day. Such conversation was as spontaneous and appropriate for any time as discussion of the latest news is today. Note that Moses called for *diligent* teaching of God's word. The Israelite parents were not to forsake their worship and teaching leadership responsibilities.

Many of the instructions given in the book of Proverbs are written as from a mother or father to a child. Perhaps the most familiar quotation related to family life is: "Train up a child in the way he should go: and when he is old, he will not depart from it" (Prov. 22:6).

Though family worship as we practice it today was not described in the Old Testament, it is in keeping with the Old
Testament charge to parents.

In early New Testament times, before the days of church
buildings, church meetings often took place in homes. (Acts
2:46; Philem. 2). Though meeting in homes may have been a
matter of necessity, this practice did continue the Old Testament image of the home as a place of worship. Paul urged
parents, fathers in particular, to raise their children "in the
nurture and admonition of the Lord" (Eph. 6:4). Paul also com-
mended young Timothy for his faith "which dwelt first in thy
grandmother Lois, and thy mother Eunice" (2 Tim. 1:5). Family
worship today continues the tradition set by early Christians.

Helps Parents Fulfill Their Role

Family worship is essential in a home if parents are to fulfill
their role—their calling—as parents. Parents cannot abdicate
or delegate their responsibility to "train up a child in the way
he should go." The biblical admonition cannot be met simply
by sending or taking the child to Sunday School. The home
still is the primary laboratory for learning. The parents' role
combines elements of pastoral and teaching tasks. While parents may feel inadequate in these elements, they are not without resources. The major purpose of this book is to guide parents in fulfilling their pastoral responsibilities as worship
leaders.

Teaches Children to Find Meaning in the
Larger Family—the Church

Just as church cannot replace the home, neither can the
home replace the church. These two divinely established insti-
tutions complement and reinforce the ministry of the other.
As the children grow up, the time will come when they will
leave the home of their parents. Some will marry and immediately establish a new home. During the initial years when the

new home is struggling for independence and identity (when the couple tries to merge the two backgrounds) the larger family of the church will help them find stability. For some grown children there will be a brief time outside a home environment (due to college, military, or work). The church fellowship will provide the needed family support. Some children will never marry, and for them the church will become a most meaningful family.

Young children and teenagers often rebel against church attendance, especially worship services. Young children often find worship services to be too restrictive in movement and too lengthy for endurance. Family worship discussion of church worship will help children to understand, appreciate, and even enjoy church services. And as children take worship leadership responsibilities at home, they naturally will develop greater understanding of the worship services at church. Even more important, they will understand how other church members can be considered as spiritual brothers and sisters—their larger family.

3
My Family Worship? How Can We Do It?

Four-year-old Donna was with her family on an extended trip out West. They had driven for hours through the flat Kansas prairie when suddenly the Colorado mountains came into view. As soon as she saw the mountains, Donna began to sing "From the mountains, to the prairies," the familiar words from "God Bless America." The words came to her mind, and she burst into song in praise of God's creation.

Donna's awe at the beauty of the mountains and her sudden but natural response was an example of spontaneous worship— one of the two basic types of worship. Spontaneous worship comes natural to children. They indulge in it instantly when they recognize some evidence of God's working in the world. The worship may be in the form of a song, or it could be a whispered exclamation, "Look at that!" It could be a giggle of delight, a shout of joy, or a silent stare of prolonged duration. The length of the worship may not be long, but it will be real. Children do not like long adult-type worship services. They prefer worship experiences which are brief, to the point, and, to some degree, entertaining. No irreverence is intended by saying that children prefer worship experiences with some degree of entertainment. For children, God is very much alive and active in their lives. He is not confined to stained-glass rituals or pew-row decorum. God is to be enjoyed. Parents who can recognize times of spontaneous worship can enter into those experiences with the child and guide the child to a deeper understanding of God.

Not all experiences of spontaneous worship are happy experiences, but they can be meaningful. Donna's parents were concerned that Donna have some knowledge about death before she suffered the shock of a relative's death. When a friend's elderly father died, Donna's parents took her to view the body at the funeral home. This was done at a time when no friends or family members were at the funeral home. Donna asked why there were flowers surrounding the casket. Her parents explained that the flowers had been placed there by people who loved the man. Donna commented, "He must have been a good man." Then followed questions about burial.

The impact of this experience was not fully evident until several months later when the family was visiting Arlington National Cemetery. As they rode in a tour bus past the thousands of stark white crosses, Donna softly chanted, "Their bodies are in the ground, but they are in heaven." Donna had grasped some meaning of eternal life.

For families to get the most out of spontaneous worship, parents must be sensitive to the opportunities for such experiences. They must be flexible enough to seize those opportunities despite prior plans or seemingly unworshipful circumstances.

Parental involvement is not optional in the second type of family worship—planned worship. Parents are the controlling agent in planned worship, regardless of whether the worship takes place at church or at home. Parents decide if and when the family will attend church and if and when home family worship will be conducted. Parents shape the children's attitude toward worship by the way they prepare for and react to church worship and the way they lead the home family worship.

Most children of all ages have difficulty deriving meaning from church services which are designed entirely for adults. The key to meaningful worship is participation. Young children who have difficulty understanding much of the abstract concepts present in sermons need to be shown ways they can reverently but actively participate in worship services. One method for preparing children for church worship is for the family to discuss the announced sermon topic. (If the topic has not been announced, perhaps the information could be obtained by calling the church office on Friday.) Discussion could be built around such questions as, What do you think the sermon will be about? What Bible stories might relate to the topic? What kind of illustrations might be used? Such questions as these create an expectant and inquisitive attitude which develops the child's listening skills. Another preparation technique is to tell the child that after the sermon you will ask the child to tell you three things that the pastor said.

During the service, the child can be guided in active, constructive participation. For example, during the song service, hold the songbook where the child can see it and point to every word as it is sung. This can be done even if the child cannot read. The child feels more a part of what is going on if he is looking at the words that the adults are singing.

Children like to doodle and draw during sermons. Why not take advantage of this favorite pastime by suggesting that the child draw church scenes? Better still, suggest that the child draw pictures which illustrate different ideas and stories presented in the sermon. The child not only is encouraged to listen but also to apply the sermon lessons to his own world of understanding. Naturally, such art work should be discussed at home following the church service.

While it may be obvious why planned worship is needed in a church, the need may not be so obvious for family worship at home. There are several reasons why it is important to have a planned structure for home worship. For example, a planned structure for worship enables the child to become familiar with the framework for worship and to feel comfortable spending a period of time within that structure. This is not to say that the structure must be rigid and inflexible. The key word is *planned*. A worship period that is planned, not just a happening, by a family will be built upon enough previous experiences that the element of familiarity will still be present even if the plan calls for spontaneous events.

Planning helps "control" the children. Planning takes into account children's ages, abilities, and interests when selecting activities and content for the worship period. Controls which are linked to age, ability, and interest are far more effective, seem less like controls, and recognize the individuality of each child more than are controls based on punishment.

Planning helps set boundaries for the children. They learn what is expected of them during the worship period. They learn that even though the family worship may consist of activities they do at other times, such as eating or playing games, that the family worship activities have a different purpose and are not to be done for an extended time. They will learn that all the activities lead toward the more sacred activities of praise and prayer.

Planning also helps to stake a claim on a certain time and place. Family worship should not be a surprise to anyone in the family. It should be looked forward to—anticipated—by each person. If everyone knows that at a future announced time the worship will take place, there will be less chance of protest because a favorite television program or commercial is on or because children are in the middle of some other fun activities. However, the constraints of staking a claim on a time apply to the parents as well as the children. Business or chance incoming telephone calls should not be allowed to infringe upon the set worship hour. Callers should be politely informed about the family worship, and arrangements made to call back. When family worship is given priority over business and social contacts, the children will realize what values are considered really important. On the contrary, if family worship must be shifted constantly because of business and social contacts, children will perceive that business and society are of higher value than worship.

Telephone calls are not the only interrupters of family worship. Drop-in visitors seem to be an excusable reason for delaying a planned worship. Again, children will learn the greater value of worship if, instead of delaying a worship period, the visitor is invited to observe and/or participate with the family. The activities could be shortened on such occasions, but the importance of worship will be magnified. Furthermore, the worship activity will provide an opportunity for further conversation and witness to the visitor. One prominent physician always included visitors in the family worship, even if the visitors were present at his invitation. In his case the children knew that bedtime was always worship time no matter what else was taking place in the house.

Staking a claim on a place for family worship is just as important as reserving a specific time for worship. Unlike a church building where the auditorium is used only for worship, every room in a house is designed and used primarily for purposes other than worship. If family members can know ahead of time where the worship will take place, they can mentally prepare themselves to regard that location as a place for worship.

Perhaps the importance of planning for family worship can best be summarized by saying that planning is preparation for holiness. The word "holy" means "set apart." Family worship is holy in that it sets apart a time, a place, selected activities, and a group of people—the family—for communion with God.

Factors Which Influence Ways of Worship at Home

Planning worship at home demands that the planners be sensitive to the many factors which influence home worship. These factors require the making of decisions—of choosing from a variety of approaches. For example, one crucial decision regarding regular family worship is how often to have the worship. Frequency of worship is a problem for some families. Many families have daily worship, but others find that daily worship, for a number of reasons, is not possible. (Saying grace at meals and reading a few verses of Scripture constitutes devotions, but not family worship as used in this book.)

Families which cannot have daily planned worship experiences should not feel guilty. Instead, they should plan worship on a frequency more suitable to all members of the family. This book is written on the premise that in families with small children, once-a-week worship will be the most likely frequency.

Frequency, be it daily, weekly, or monthly, implies regularity. More important than how often is how regular and consistent are you. It is better to have a definite weekly worship than to have a daily worship which is subject to constant modifications and cancellations to fit into the schedule of each unique day.

Other factors which will influence the ways of worship are time of day selected and the length of time available. Obviously the time of day chosen for family worship must be a time when all the family can be together and when there is ample time for total family involvement. Breakfast time would seem to be an ideal time if all the family members are on a schedule which permits them to eat together. However, few families would find ample time either before or after breakfast for an unhurried worship period. There is a danger that any regular mealtime family worship will become routine ritual just like the meals.

The frequency of family worship will have a bearing on the length of worship. Daily worship observances will dictate a shorter period of time for worship. A weekly schedule will allow a longer, more flexible family worship fellowship.

Of equal importance is the setting and location for worship. Almost any place inside the house would be suitable for some type of family worship. If the worship theme is on God's provision of our daily needs such as food, the kitchen would be an appropriate location. A worship based on the creation story could take place in the workshop, where things are made, or outside under the stars.

There are certain advantages to conducting the family worship in different places around the home. One advantage is that changing the worship locations demonstrates that God can be worshiped anywhere. Furthermore, worshiping in different places makes those places holy—sets them apart. Children especially like for worship to be held in their own bedrooms.

The advantage of conducting family worship in the same location each time is that the child will come to associate that location with worship. Consequently, upon nearing the location the child will be more in the worship frame of mind.

Still another influence on worship is the worship aids available. Some people will use no aids other than the Bible. Others will use Bible dictionaries, commentaries, maps, and pictures to help understand and/or illustrate the focal Scripture passage. Such aids lead children to realize that the Bible is not just a book of the past—that the stories and lessons to be learned are just as relevant for today as they were thousands of years ago.

Perhaps no factor must be given more consideration in planning family worship than the age of the child or children. At no time should the worship leader treat the children as inferior or limited in understanding. However, the leader should be aware of age-difference learning characteristics. The younger the child, the more he or she tends to think and talk only in concrete terms. The younger child is not able to think and converse in terms of abstract concepts. Many an adult who has waxed eloquent on some subject such as the Holy Spirit has been surprised to hear children later talk of God as being a ghost. For younger children the world is a place of absolutes. Worship services aimed at their age group should concentrate on Bible facts. Services planned for older children can deal more with abstract themes such as doctrines.

Coupled in importance with the age of children is the number of children in a family. Each additional person adds another dimension to the worship hour. Another person contributes insights while, at the same time, learning. Each person should have a designated opportunity to lead part of the worship and should be allowed to inject spontaneous comments and questions. In families with more than one child, there will be times when the children compete for the right to ask a question, make a statement, or lead an activity. This can result in charges of "Unfair," "It's my turn," "Please let me say this one thing"— all of which may seem counterproductive as far as worship is concerned. However, a lively exchange of ideas also can result in siblings leading each other to a deeper understanding of God's truths. In one-child families, the child will not have to compete for attention, but the parents may need to raise questions the child does not think of in order to stimulate the child and to broaden his concept of God.

The single greatest influence on a family worship service is the attitude of the worship leader. If the leader has a set pattern which must be followed, then home worship will become routine—a ritual which is meaningful only to the person who controls it. If the leader allows all family members to participate to the best of their ability and is creative in planning the worship, then family worship will be a dynamic spiritual experience.

Essential Elements for Meaningful Family Worship

There are as many ways to conduct a home worship service as there are families and as there are occasions for worship. No family will conduct a worship service just like the one previously conducted. Even if the family set out to repeat exactly a home service, the change in time and the experiences encountered will make the second service different from the first. These changing characteristics of a worship service should be of no concern, actually they should be preferred. Each home service should be fresh and exciting, not a mere repetition of a past service.

Though each service will and should have distinctive differences, some being even less uplifting than others, there are some elements which should be included to ensure that the services are meaningful. Not all of these elements are essential for each service. Neither are they essential for other types of worship such as church worship. However, for family worship to be meaningful, ensure that the following elements are included.

Family members of all ages should participate and contribute. No one should be left out because he is too young. Even an infant can be included by placing the baby in the family circle. To have genuine *family* worship, everyone in the family must be included.

This does not mean that family worship can't be held if a member of the family is missing. Even if the father is away on a business trip or an older child is away at camp, the worship should be continued on the regular schedule. The missing person still can be a part of the worship by being remembered in prayer.

Food should be included. Even in Old Testament times, long before the institution of the Lord's Supper, partaking of a meal together was a spiritual event. The eating of the meal should be treated as part of the service and not incidental to watching a television show at the same time. Eating is the one thing family members of all ages can participate in equally in enjoyment and ability. It is one experience which puts all members on an equal basis.

Games should be included as a means of involving children. Including games is a concession to the child, not just for their enjoyment but to permit the adult to step into the child's world. Play is as much the child's occupation as is housekeeping for the mother or going to the shop is for the father. For the parents to participate in play is to show that they understand and care for the child's viewpoint. In a figurative sense, through playing together the parents and child join heart and hands and move easily from the sharing-in-fun situation to a sharing-in-faith situation. Participating in games allows the child to enter into the worship experience through the doorway of his own frame of reference rather than being forced to enter the worship experience through the prescribed structure of the adult.

Games provide a means for getting in tune with the child's

energies and for channeling that energy from physical expression to mental and spiritual experience. It is not fair that a child who has been very active, suddenly has to sit quietly. Not only is it not fair, it is not a good way to introduce him to worship. To draw a sharp distinctive between fun activity and worship activity is to convey the idea that fun or happiness is not to be associated with God. Children learn as much about theology and doctrine through insinuation as they do through instruction. What they learn through instruction they eventually perceive to be the ideal concept of faith. The ideal is to be held up, to be acknowledged. The ideal is to be pursued but with the awareness that it really can't be achieved. What children learn through insinuation they eventually perceive to be the practical, attainable concept of faith. The integration of faith-activities and fun-activities for the family is not sacrilegious. It is, rather, a merging of learning-by-instruction and learning-by-insinuation, which, from the child's viewpoint, validates the entire experience—makes it genuine and worthy of applying to life.

The Bible is a must. Every family worship service must include focus on the Bible. However, this does not mean that a Scripture text must be found to justify each worship experience. God, through the Holy Spirit, can reveal spiritual truths to individuals in many ways. Yet the Bible is the revealed authority of God by which all other revelations should be tested. Using the Bible in worship teaches the child and reaffirms for the parent that the Bible is the primary source of information about God, the divinely inspired record of his work on earth, and the authoritative guide for Christian living.

The Bible can be included in a worship service in such ways as:

—placing the Bible in the center of the gathering and making the Bible the interest center;

—leading the family to memorize a verse of Scripture;

—playing a Bible game;

—sharing favorite Bible verses;

—telling Bible stories; or

—acting out Bible stories.

Prayer is another essential element for family worship. For many people it may seem that prayer, like the Bible, should be an obvious part of worship. Both prayer and the Bible are included in this listing to ensure that they are not taken for granted and to emphasize that they are essential for meaningful family worship. Some individuals claim to commune with God simply by looking at the natural world he created or by listening to inspirational music. While we may sense God's presence through nature and music, prayer is the only channel God has provided for us to communicate with him—the channel for expression of praise or petition for pardon. Meaningful communication with God is a deliberate, thoughtful message from the heart, not an euphoric feeling.

Questions—unique to family worship. There are some distinctive elements in family worship which are not usually found in other forms of worship. Food and games are obviously two of those elements. Another distinctive element is questions. The type and complexity of questions asked will depend upon the age of the child or children in the family. Questions help children to recall events in a story, to interpret meanings, and to make application. Questions also enable parents to lead children to grasp the basic teaching of a story, a song, or a verse of Scripture. Children love questions, because questions are a mental game of hide-and-seek, a game of clues and discovery. They delight in giving answers.

Discussion—another family worship distinctive. Discussion will naturally follow questions asked by the parents. A time for discussion allows children to ask their own questions. It encourages them to think for themselves, to probe for answers. It teaches them that God's truths can withstand even the most searching questions. Discussion will clear up misunderstandings and pave the way for new insights for both parents and children.

Time—the most essential element. Time must be allowed

for food, games, Bible, prayer, questions, discussion, and the total family worship experience. Family worship which is under a time constraint of five, ten, or even fifteen minutes is worship which limits the blessings to be received. There is danger that the worship leader will be more concerned with completing planned activities within the time limitation than in allowing a worship experience to take place. In keeping with the admonition of a favorite hymn, the family worship leader must "Take time to be holy," to be set apart in worship.

A Format for Family Worship

Following is an explanation of the format for family worship as suggested in this book. Worship leaders should not hesitate to modify the format to suit individual family preferences.

Food Suggestion: Throughout the first two chapters of this book, emphasis has been placed on the importance of beginning the family worship experience with the "breaking of bread." In most cases, the food suggestion will be for some type of snack rather than a complete meal. Remember that this is one time where fun food may take precedence over nourishment. When possible, the food suggestion will tie in with the theme subject. Suggestions will be limited to readily available items, though some special menus may be included. No attempt has been made to make each food suggestion different. On the contrary, food suggestions are often repeated for the benefit and ease of those who follow the suggestions exactly.

Action Activity: This will consist of a game or exercise designed to channel the energies of the child, and to create a sense of fellowship for the entire family. It is important that the entire family participate in the action activity.

Song Time: Occasionally specific songs will be suggested, but families should select those songs with which they are most familiar. The purpose of song time is to provide a transition from the action activity to the worship activity. Song time should begin with fast, lively songs, and conclude with quieter songs and hymns. One or more family songbooks, perhaps like

ones used in children's departments at church, would be a
good investment.

Interest Item   (optional): In some worship experiences it will
be helpful to provide a selected item which will create curiosity
about the subject and/or which will illustrate a specific point.
An interest item will not be needed for each worship experience.

Listening Preparation Questions: One or two questions
will be suggested for asking prior to reading the story and
Scripture passage. The questions will be tips to the children
on what they should be listening for.

Story: The story will be the heart of the experience. Children will identify with someone in the story, and will make
application to their own situation. The story creates a hypothet-
ical situation which the child can visualize and "observe" from
an impartial viewpoint. Being an "observer" allows the child
to "try out" possible solutions to typical or representative problems and situations.

Story Questions: Questions are suggested as a means to
review what the children have heard, to focus on key portions
of the content, and to stimulate discussion.

Scripture Passage: The Scripture is given following the
story as a means of teaching children to turn to the Bible for
guidance when dealing with life situations. Some parents may
want to follow the more traditional practice of reading the
Scripture passage prior to the story. Still others may choose
to read from the Bible prior to the story and then repeat it
following the story.

Scripture Question: The Scripture question teaches the
child to ask "What does it mean?" about all Scripture. Only
through learning what a Scripture passage means can a child
apply the lesson to life.

Scripture Comment for Parents: This section will consist
of a brief explanation of the Scripture passage. The comment
is intended to aid the parent in summarizing the meaning of
the passage. The comment is *not* to be read to the children.

Prayer Suggestion: Families will want to supplement the suggestions with prayer for friends and family members.

Follow-up Activity: This optional activity is one way to extend the worship experience beyond the family worship time. The activity could be begun immediately following the family worship hour, or it could be done at some other time. Whenever the child engages in the activity, even days later, it will remind him of the worship experience and thus will reinforce that experience.

4
Patterns for Weekly Worship at Home

Favorite Bible Events

MIRACLE ON THE MOUNTAIN

Food Suggestion: Use picnic food.

Action Activity: Have a cracker-eating contest. Give each family member a cracker. Each person must run across the room to a designated chair, eat their cracker, whistle (or blow if they can't whistle yet), and run back. The person with the fastest time wins.

Song Time: Include a singing blessing or grace.

Interest Item: Small loaf of bread.

Listening Preparation Question: What did the boy have to eat?

Story: "Mother, Mother," yelled the boy, as he dashed through the door of his home.

"Oh, there you are, Son," said his mother. "I was getting worried. You've been gone since early this morning. I heard that a crowd of people had some sort of meeting up on the mountain. I know you like to play on the mountain, and I was afraid all the people there might have frightened you."

"But, Mother, I was with the crowd," panted the boy, still out of breath.

"I might have known. You can tell me more about it later. It's almost time to eat, and you need to wash your hands. I imagine that you are hungry. Did you eat all the bread and the fish you took with you this morning?"

"I not only ate it, I helped feed the crowd," said the boy.

Mother laughed, "It was nice of you to share your food, but I don't imagine it lasted long."

"Mother, you don't understand. The food I had fed everyone in the crowd. It was a miracle done by Jesus!"

"Maybe I'd better stop what I'm doing and let you tell me what happened."

The boy sat on the floor facing his mother. "When I saw the crowd gathering, I decided to see what was going on. I pushed my way up to the center of the group, and there was Jesus teaching. I tried to get even closer when I bumped into the disciple they call Andrew. I thought he would make me leave. Instead he just smiled and helped me get closer. He did ask me how much food I had, and I told him I had five loaves and two fish."

"Surely he must have laughed at such a small amount," said the boy's mother.

"No, not at all," the boy answered. "He just thanked me, and then he talked with Jesus. And before I realized it, Jesus was walking toward me. He put his hand on my shoulder and asked if he could use the food to feed the people."

"What did you say?" asked the mother.

"I didn't know what to say, so I didn't say anything. I just handed the bread and fish to him."

"You should have said something, but then what happened?"

"Jesus prayed over the food, and then the disciples started giving it to the people seated on the ground. I don't understand how, but there was enough food for everyone. There even was a lot of food left over."

"I'm proud of you, Son," said the mother, "because even though you didn't have much food, you were willing to share all that you had with others. Jesus took the little you had and used it to bless many people."

Story Questions: Where had the boy been? Why did the mother laugh when the boy said that he helped feed the crowd? What disciple did the boy meet on the mountain? Who did Andrew tell about the boy's food? What did Jesus do with the food?

Scripture Passage: "There is a lad here, which hath five barley loaves, and two small fishes: but what are they among so many?" (John 6:9).

Scripture Question: Why did the disciples think that the boy's food was not enough?

Scripture Comment for Parents: The Bible states that the group gathered on the mountain consisted of five thousand men. If there were women present, the crowd was much larger. No wonder the disciples felt that five barley loaves and two fish were not enough. Jesus gave thanks for the food available and then proceeded to feed the entire group. When everyone had eaten all that they wanted, the leftovers were gathered into baskets. Twelve baskets of leftover bread were collected. The little boy had been willing to give all that he had, and with Jesus' help, what he gave resulted in a miracle.

Prayer Suggestion: Ask God that your family be willing to share with persons in need.

Follow-up Activity: If your church has a pantry for the needy, you might want to visit it with your family. Let each child take a can of food he or she personally selected from your own pantry.

MIRIAM THINKS FAST

Food Suggestion: Include foods from Bible times, such as honey, dried fruit, and dark bread.

Action Activity: Have a boat race. Place a dishpan filled with water on the table. Give each family member a small wooden or stick boat. Race each other across the pan by blowing boats from opposite sides of the dishpan.

Song Time: Include a song of faith, such as "My Faith Looks Up to Thee."

Interest Item: Baby blanket.

Listening Preparation Question: What was used to make the baby's basket?

Story: Miriam was scared. She could see the covered basket containing her little brother floating near the bank of the river. She knew that the basket would stay afloat because she had been watching it all morning. But she was scared just thinking about what might happen to her brother when someone found the basket.

The Pharaoh of Egypt, where Miriam lived, had made a rule that all boy babies born to Hebrews were to be thrown into the river and drowned. The Pharaoh was afraid that someday there would be more Hebrew men than Egyptian men in the country, and that the Hebrews would take over. Killing all the Hebrew boy babies was one way the Pharaoh could make sure the Egyptians would continue controlling the country.

Miriam's brother, Moses, was three months old, and her mother had kept Moses hidden ever since he had been born. It wasn't long though before Moses became too large to keep hidden at home. His mother was afraid someone would hear him cry and the soldiers would come and take Moses away.

Then Moses' mother had an idea. She would put Moses into the river in her own way. She and Miriam had gathered a large supply of bulrushes to make a special basket. Bulrushes were reeds which grew in swampy places. Miriam had watched as her mother skillfully wove the strips of reed together. Then her mother had covered the outside of the basket with some gooey stuff she called pitch. "This," her mother had said, "will keep the water out and the basket will float."

Finally, Mother and Miriam had wrapped Moses snugly so he couldn't wave his arms and turn the basket over. And very carefully they had placed him in the basket.

Just before sunup Miriam and her mother had crept out of the house. When they got to the river, Miriam's mother had waded in with the basket and placed it in the midst of a thicket of reeds. Then Miriam's mother had told Miriam to hide where she could watch the basket.

Miriam had watched for a long time, and nothing had happened. Suddenly she heard voices coming down the path along the river. The voices were all girls' voices. "At least there are no soldiers coming," thought Miriam, as she relaxed a little. But her heart almost stopped when the people came into view.

Her mother had made a terrible mistake! The spot they had chosen to place Moses was right where the Pharaoh's daughter came to bathe!

It was too late for Miriam to get to her mother. She watched in horror as Pharaoh's daughter spotted the basket almost immediately and sent one of the girls with her to get the basket.

Miriam could hear Moses begin to cry when the Pharaoh's daughter opened the basket. The princess picked up Moses and tried to comfort him. When Miriam realized that the princess would not harm Moses, she had an idea. Quickly she ran from her hiding place.

"Would you like for me to get one of the Hebrew women to take care of the baby?" she asked.

"Oh, yes," was the reply.

Miriam ran as fast as she could and brought back her mother. Then Pharaoh's daughter said to Miriam's mother, "Take care of this child for me, and I will pay you for your work."

Thanks to Miriam's quick thinking, Moses was able to grow up to be a leader of the Hebrew people.

Story Questions: What was Miriam doing? Why was her brother in a basket? Why did the Pharaoh want to kill Hebrew baby boys? Why did Pharaoh's daughter come to the river? What did the princess do when she found Moses in the basket? What was Miriam's good idea? Who was hired to take care of Moses? What did Moses grow up to become?

Scripture Passage: "By faith Moses, when he was born, was hid three months of his parents, because they saw he was a proper child; and they were not afraid of the king's commandments." (Heb. 11:23).

Scripture Question: Were Moses' parents brave? Why?

Scripture Comment: It took much faith in God for Moses' parents to disobey the Pharaoh. They knew that they would be in a lot of trouble if anyone found out what they had done. Yet they trusted God to take care of them. Their faith in God was far more powerful than any fear they may have had of the Pharaoh.

Prayer Suggestion: Pray that God will help you to have strong faith in him like Moses' parents did.

Follow-up Activity: Act out the story. Use as many characters as you have family members.

THE BOY AND THE GIANT

Food Suggestion: Bread and cheese.

Action Activity: Arm wrestle—Give smaller children the advantage of using both arms.

Song Time: Include a song of faith, such as "Have Faith in God."

Interest Item: Five smooth stones.

Listening Preparation Question: What did David take to his brothers?

Story: "David, do you have all the food ready to go?" asked Jesse, his father.

David looked over the container of parched corn, the ten loaves of bread, and the ten cheeses. "Yes, father," he said, "it's all ready."

"Good," said Jesse. "Take the food to the camp where your brothers are staying with the other Israelite soldiers."

David was too young to join the army, but his three eldest brothers had gone with King Saul and other Israelite men to fight against the Philistine army.

David arrived at the camp early in the morning just as the Israelite army was lining up for battle. While David was talking with his brothers, a Philistine soldier walked toward the Israelite army. David did not notice the Philistine until the man shouted. When David looked up, he realized he was looking at the biggest man he had ever seen. The Philistine soldier was a giant who wore heavy metal clothing all over his body. He was a very frightening sight.

The giant, whose name was Goliath, roared to the Israelite soldiers, "There is no need for all your soldiers to go into battle. Just pick out one man to fight me. If he beats me, then all the Philistines will serve you. But, if I beat him, all of the Israelites must serve us."

The Israelites were scared. Not one Israelite soldier dared step forward to challenge the giant. Instead, everyone ran away from him.

David couldn't believe what he saw—Israelite soldiers running from one man. "Won't someone stand up to this Philistine who defies the army of God?" exclaimed David. The more David talked, the more it sounded like he was willing to fight the giant himself. David's older brother, Eliab, was embarrassed by his little brother's boasts. Eliab became angry with David and tried to keep him quiet. But David continued to talk about fighting Goliath.

Some of the soldiers told King Saul about David. And the king sent for David. Standing before the king, David declared: "No one should be afraid of this giant. I will go fight Goliath."

"But you are just a youth," said Saul, "and Goliath is an experienced soldier."

David then told the king about how, as a shepherd, he had fought with a lion and a bear. Then David said, "The Lord that helped me defeat the lion and the bear will help me defeat this Philistine."

King Saul realized that David really trusted God to help defeat the Philistine. The king agreed to let David fight on behalf of the Israelite army. Saul even offered to let David wear his own armor into battle. David tried on the King's heavy metal clothing, but it was so big and heavy that David couldn't move.

"I can't wear these," said David, "I'm not used to them." David took off the metal clothing and picked up his shepherd's stick. Quickly he gathered five smooth stones, and with his sling ready, he walked toward Goliath, the giant.

David paid no attention to Goliath's comments about him being a mere boy. He simply said: "You want to fight with a spear and a sword. I come in the name of the Lord. God will

help me defeat you, and all the world will know about the
God of Israel." Then David placed one of the smooth stones
in his sling and hurled the stone at the giant. The stone hit
Goliath between the eyes, and the giant fell to the ground.
The Israelite soldiers shouted praises, while the Philistine army
ran in fear. They all realized that God had helped a young
boy defeat the mighty Goliath.

Story Questions: In what army were David's brothers serving? What army were they fighting? What was the giant's
name? What did the giant want to do? What did the Israelite
soldiers think of Goliath? What did David volunteer to do?
Why did David's oldest brother become angry with him? Why
didn't David wear Saul's armor? Why did David choose to use
the sling? Who did David say would help him to defeat the
giant?

Scripture Passage: "David said moreover, The Lord that
delivered me out of the paw of the lion, and out of the paw
of the bear, he will deliver me out of the hand of this Philistine"
(1 Sam. 17:37).

Scripture Question: What do you think David meant when
he said that the Lord would "deliver" him out of the "hand"
of the Philistine?

Scripture Comments for Parents: As a shepherd, David believed that God had protected him and had given him the
ability to kill the wild animals when he was alone watching
the sheep. David had tremendous faith in God. He had no
reason to doubt that God would take care of him in the battle
with the giant. God is consistent in his watchcare over those
who trust in him.

Prayer Suggestion: Ask God to help you trust him completely when you need his help and protection.

Follow-up Activity: Draw a frieze to tell the story. A frieze
is a series of pictures arranged on a long strip of paper so
that they tell a continuous story. Decide who will draw each
portion of the story. Include parents' drawings as well as children's.

Roadside Rescue

Food Suggestion: Plan food that a sick person might eat, such as soup or toast.

Action Activity: If your family group includes three or more, play "musical chairs." The older name for this game is "going to Jerusalem."

Song Time: Include a song of courage, such as "Mine Eyes Have Seen the Glory."

Interest Item: First-aid supplies.

Listening Preparation Question: Why was the traveler frightened when he heard footsteps?

Story: "I wish I didn't have to walk by myself on this trip," thought the traveler, as he walked on the road between Jericho and Jerusalem. "Many people have been robbed on this road. I'll have to be careful." Just that moment he felt a sharp pain in the back of his head. The pain was so bad that he fell to his knees. Then he saw a huge rock coming right at him, but it was too late to duck. The last thing he remembered thinking was that the robbers were going to kill him.

Some time later the traveler slowly regained consciousness. His head hurt so much that he couldn't move it, and his body ached all over where the robbers must have beaten him. All the traveler could do was lay there and groan.

It wasn't long before the traveler heard footsteps on the road. At first he was frightened, thinking perhaps the robbers had come back to make certain that he was dead. His fear quickly changed to hope when he recognized the clothing of a religious leader. The traveler opened his mouth to ask for help, but all he could do was make a groaning sound. When the religious leader heard the groan and saw the wounded traveler, he quickly moved to the other side of the road and hurried out of sight.

Some time later the traveler heard someone else coming down the road. When the person came closer, the traveler realized that this man belonged to a group of people called

Levites. The Levites performed special tasks in the Temple. Surely this man would help him. But the Levite took one look at the wounded traveler and also hurried by.

The next noise the traveler heard was the braying of a donkey. When the donkey came into view, the traveler saw that the rider of the donkey was a Samaritan. "Oh no," thought the traveler, "I'll get no help from this man. I'm a Jew, and Samaritans never have anything to do with Jews." But much to the traveler's surprise, the Samaritan ran to him as soon as he saw him. The Samaritan gave the traveler a drink and poured some liquids over his body which made the traveler feel better. Then the Samaritan placed the traveler on the donkey, and they went down the road until they found an inn where they could spend the night.

The next day the Samaritan had to leave, but the traveler still hurt too much to leave. The traveler didn't have any money to pay for staying at the inn since the robbers had taken all he had. The Samaritan gave the innkeeper some money and said: "Here is money to pay for taking care of this man. If the cost of caring for him comes to more than what I have given you, I'll pay you the rest when I return." And the traveler stayed at the inn until he was well enough to go home.

Story Questions: What happened to the traveler as he walked down the road? Who could have helped the traveler but didn't? Why do you think the religious leader and the Levite hurried past the wounded man? Why did the wounded man think that the Samaritan would not help him? What did the Samaritan do to help?

Scripture Passage: "Which now of these three, thinkest thou, was neighbour unto him that fell among the thieves? And he said, He that shewed mercy on him. Then said Jesus unto him, Go, and do thou likewise" (Luke 10:36-37).

Scripture Question: What was Jesus saying that we ought to do?

Scripture Comment for Parents: Jesus told the story of the good Samaritan in response to the question, Who is my neighbor? The story illustrates the fact that our neighbor is not just the person who lives next door or not just someone we know. Our neighbor is anyone in need. We become good neighbors when we do something to meet the needs of other people.

Prayer Suggestion: Ask God to give you courage to help others.

Follow-up Activity: Make paper-bag puppets of all the characters in the parable. Put on a puppet show. You may wish to invite neighbor children who do not attend church.

THE LION TAMER

Food Suggestion: Plan simple, healthful foods which Daniel might have chosen, such as fruit, cheese, or nuts.

Action Activity: "Pat and Rub." Pat stomach with one hand and rub head with the other. Leader calls out changes and adds footwork, depending on dexterity of children involved.

Song Time: Include the "Doxology."

Interest Item: Picture of a lion.

Listening Preparation Question: What did Daniel do every day?

Story: The newly appointed rulers of Babylon were angry. King Darius had selected Daniel to be the chief ruler.

"Why should Daniel be chief over us?" said one of the rulers. "After all, he was not born in this country. He was brought here years ago when our nation captured Jerusalem."

"Yes," said another ruler, "he is from another country. He also worships the God of the Israelites rather than one of our gods."

A third ruler spoke up, "I've heard that the king chose him simply because he has 'an excellent spirit' in him."

"I don't know what that means," said the first ruler, "but I do know we must do something to get rid of him."

The rulers tried to find ways to make Daniel look bad in the eyes of the king. As much as they tried, they could not find one thing against him.

Finally they had an idea they thought would work. First, the Babylonian rulers tricked King Darius into signing a law. The law said that people could only pray to the king. Then they watched to see what Daniel would do.

Just as they thought, Daniel did exactly the same thing he had done every day. He went to his room, stood at the windows which faced Jerusalem, and prayed to God.

King Darius was greatly upset when the rulers told him they had seen Daniel praying to God. Darius was not upset with Daniel, but he realized he had been tricked by the rulers. There was nothing he could do. Once a law was made not even the king could change it. Darius had to place Daniel in the lions' den as punishment for praying to God.

Early the next morning the king hurried to the place where Daniel had been thrown into the lions' den. He shouted down into the den, "Daniel, has your God been able to save you from the lions?"

And Daniel answered back, "O king, my God sent his angel and shut the lions' mouth, and they have not hurt me. My God protected me because I had done no wrong."

King Darius was happy that Daniel was not hurt, and he ordered that Daniel be released from the den. The king realized that Daniel's God was great and powerful. From that time on, the king wanted everyone to worship the true God just like Daniel.

Story Questions: Why were the rulers angry? Why did they not want Daniel to be chief ruler next to the king? What did the rulers get the king to do? What did they do after the king signed the new law? What did the king have to do with Daniel? What did the king find when he went to the lions' den the next morning? What did the king learn about God?

Scripture Passage: "He kneeled upon his knees three times a day, and prayed, and gave thanks before his God" (Dan. 6:10).

Scripture Question: What was one thing Daniel always said to God when he prayed?

Scripture Comment for Parents: Daniel always gave thanks to God when he prayed. Daniel had much for which to be thankful. For one thing, he could be thankful that God was powerful enough to protect him in a foreign country. He could be thankful that God had made him a ruler, but most of all Daniel could be thankful that God had more power than even the king. No wonder Daniel prayed three times a day. He had so much for which to be thankful.

Prayer Suggestion: Thank God for giving you food, clothing, a home, and people to love.

Follow-up Activity: Make a list of things for which you and your family are thankful. Keep the list in a handy place and add to it each day for one week.

THE HOUSE GUEST

Food Suggestion: Something you usually prepare only for guests.

Action Activity: Make an obstacle course using chairs, tables, stools, and so forth. Time each person's run. Run the course a second time so that each person can compete against his own record.

Song Time: Include a song about Zacchaeus.

Interest Item: Money.

Listening Preparation Question: Why did people become angry with Zacchaeus?

Story: "What's going on?" asked Zacchaeus. "What's all the noise about?" It had been a peaceful day in Jericho until just a few minutes ago. Of course, some people had become angry with Zacchaeus earlier and had shouted at him, but that happened every day. As the chief tax collector, Zacchaeus often made people angry. He had become rich by making some people pay more taxes than they really owed.

By now people were running past Zacchaeus toward the main street. Zacchaeus grabbed the arm of a man hurrying by and asked again, "What's going on?"

The man hardly paid any attention to Zacchaeus. He quickly pulled away but shouted back over his shoulder: "It's Jesus, Jesus of Nazareth. He's passing through the city."

Immediately, Zacchaeus became as excited as all the people around him. He had heard much about Jesus—about his unusual teachings and about miracles he had performed. Zacchaeus decided that he, too, must see Jesus. And he hurried along with the crowd.

When Zacchaeus got to the main street, he could tell by the cheers that Jesus was passing by. But Zacchaeus couldn't see Jesus. Zacchaeus was too short to see over the heads of other people, and now the crowd was so thick that there was no way he could push through to see Jesus.

Suddenly Zacchaeus had an idea. He rushed along the edge of the crowd down the street in the direction in which Jesus was walking. Soon Zacchaeus was ahead of the crowd, but he kept on going until he came to a sycamore tree. Quickly, he climbed up into the tree. Now he would be able to look down and see Jesus despite the crowd.

Within a few minutes Jesus was walking directly under the tree where Zacchaeus was. Much to his surprise, Jesus looked up into the tree and said, "Zacchaeus, come down quickly. I want to spend the day at your house."

Happily Zacchaeus led Jesus to his home. Then he listened as Jesus talked about how to live like God wanted. Zacchaeus believed all that Jesus taught. Zacchaeus decided that he, too, would become a follower of Jesus. He stood and said: "My Lord, I will give half of what I have to the poor, Also, if I have cheated anyone on their taxes, I will pay them back four times as much as what I took."

Jesus smiled and said, "Today salvation has come to this house."

Story Questions: What was Zacchaeus' job? What was causing all the excitement in Jericho? Why did Zacchaeus have difficulty seeing Jesus? What did he do in order to see Jesus?

How did Jesus surprise Zacchaeus? What did Zacchaeus decide to do?

Scripture Passage: "And Jesus said unto him, This day is salvation come to this house" (Luke 19:9).

Scripture Question: To whom was Jesus talking when he made this statement?

Scripture Comment for Parents: When a person accepts Jesus as their Savior, other people should be able to tell that he now lives for Jesus. When Jesus heard Zacchaeus tell all that he would do to help the poor and to pay back the persons he had cheated, Jesus knew that Zacchaeus truly believed in him. Zacchaeus did not receive salvation because of the good things he promised to do. He promised to do good things because he had received salvation through Jesus Christ.

Prayer Suggestion: Pray that everyone in your home will accept Christ as his Savior.

Follow-up Activity: Find a climbing tree and let children pretend they are Zacchaeus watching over the crowds for Jesus.

GRANDFATHER'S BOAT

Food Suggestion: Include foods you would use if you were going on a long trip, such as dried fruit and meat sticks.

Action Activity: Play charades, guessing animals.

Song Time: Not all the songs sung during worship have to be hymn-type songs. You might enjoy singing rounds such as "Row, Row, Row Your Boat."

Interest Item: Picture or drawing of a rainbow.

Listening Preparation Question: How many animals of each kind were placed on the ark?

Story: "Tell me about Grandfather and the boat," said Canaan.

"But, Son," said Ham, "I've told you that story many times."

"I know, Father," said Canaan, "but since it all happened before I was born, I want to hear about it again. I want to be certain that I know everything that happened so when I grow up and have children, I can tell them about what happened to you, Uncle Japheth, Uncle Shem, and of course, to Grandfather Noah."

"All right, Son," laughed Ham, "I'll tell you again. Many years ago the people of the world were evil. They continually did things that displeased God. But one man and his family lived like God wanted people to live, and that person was your Grandfather Noah. So when God decided to punish the wicked people by sending a flood, he told Grandfather Noah to build a huge boat."

"I remember," shouted Canaan, "the boat was called an ark, and it was made of gopher wood!"

"Right," said Ham, "God told Grandfather Noah to gather two each of some animals and seven each of others. When the animals had been loaded, all of our family got on board and shut the door."

"Then came the rain," exclaimed Canaan.

"Soon you will be telling me the story," chuckled Ham. "Yes, it rained for forty days and forty nights. And when the rain stopped, water covered the earth. We were not able to leave the ark as soon as the rain stopped. We had to wait until the waters got low enough for us to walk on earth. We stayed on the ark almost eleven months."

"Eleven months! Wow!" said Canaan. "Now tell me the part about the rainbow," he added, excitedly.

"I will," replied Ham, "but let me remind you that one of the first things Grandfather Noah did after we left the ark was to build an altar and worship God. Then God promised that never again would he send a flood to punish people. He gave us the rainbow as a sign to let us know that he would always keep his promise."

"Tell the story again, Father," begged Canaan.

"Not now," replied Ham smiling, "and the next time I'm going to let you tell the story to me."

"Oh no!" exclaimed Canaan, as he ran off to play.

Story Questions: Who was Canaan's grandfather? Can you name one of his uncles? What kind of wood was used to make the ark? How long was Noah and his family on the ark? What did Noah do when he got off the ark? What does the rainbow mean?

Scripture Passage: "But Noah found grace in the eyes of the Lord" (Gen. 6:8).

Scripture Question: Does this verse mean that God was pleased or displeased with Noah?

Scripture Comment for Parents: All the people of the world in the time of Noah were wicked. They were so wicked that God planned to destroy the people of earth. But Noah was the only person in the world who was obedient to God. God saw Noah, along with his family, as one person whom he would not destroy with the wicked people of the world. God told Noah what to do to avoid destruction. Noah believed God and followed his instructions, even though it must have looked silly to be building such a large boat on dry land.

Prayer Suggestion: Pray for people who don't believe in God or who don't obey him. Ask God to help you be obedient to him.

Follow-up Activity: Look at a prism or diamond ring. See how many different colors you can see.

Growing in Faith

THE PING-PONG PROBLEM

Food Suggestion: Brownies.

Action Activity: Try a variety of games with a Ping-Pong ball. Play Ping-Pong baseball, batting with your hand and using different items of furniture as bases. Or, place a Ping-Pong ball in the center of a table with family members stationed around the edge of the table. Each person tries to blow the ball off the table in an area where someone else is standing.

Song Time: Let each family member choose a song.

Interest Item: A Ping-Pong ball and paddle.

Listening Preparation Question: Who was afraid of being called a baby?

Story: "I will be late getting home from work today, Chip," said Mrs. Russell. "I want you to come right home from school, stay in the house, and do your homework."

"OK, Mom," Chip said, finishing his milk and running out the door.

That afternoon on his way home from school, Chip was invited by Mike, one of the big boys, to play on his new Ping-Pong table.

"No," said Chip, "Mom told me to go right home."

"Oh, come on to my house for a few minutes," said Mike. "She'll never know, Don't be a baby."

Chip didn't know what to do. He wanted to go to Mike's house. If he didn't go Mike would invite someone else. And he wanted to be Mike's best friend.

"Oh, OK," said Chip, "just for a little while."

Chip and Mike had lots of fun playing Ping-Pong. And Mike's mother had made brownies for them to eat. Soon it was almost dark.

"I've got to get home!" said Chip, looking out the window. "If I leave now, I can still beat Mom home and she'll never know." Chip ran as fast as he could. He barely made it to his room as his mother came in the front door.

"If you have finished your homework, we can go out and eat and maybe go get your new shoes," said Mrs. Russell smiling.

Chip, still a bit breathless, stuttered, "Oh, yes, Mother, I have been finished for thirty minutes."

Chip realized that he had disobeyed his mother, and now he had lied to cover up his actions. Chip didn't feel very good.

Story Questions: What was Chip supposed to do after school? What was special about Mike? What did Mike say to persuade Chip to play with him instead of going home? Why did Chip feel bad when his mother came home? How did the story make you feel? Did you feel guilty? Have you ever done anything wrong and then not told the truth about it?

Scripture Passage: "I said, I will confess my transgressions unto the Lord; and thou forgavest the iniquity of my sin" (Ps. 32:5).

Scripture Question: What does it mean to "confess"?

Scripture Comment for Parents: This verse comes from a psalm written by a man who tried to keep secret something he had done wrong. As long as he refused to tell God about his wrongdoing, he felt very sick. Finally he felt so bad that he decided to confess his wrongdoing to God; that is, he admitted to God that he had done something bad. When the man said he was sorry for what he did, God forgave him.

God did not make the man ill. The man felt bad because he knew that he was disobeying God. He felt guilty. He felt good again only after confessing his sin and being forgiven.

Prayer Suggestion: Thank God for forgiving our sins when we confess them to him. Ask him to help us to be obedient at all times.

Follow-up Activity: Act out the story three times—one time just as it is written, another time act out how Chip should have responded to Mike's invitation, and then act out how Chip should have responded to his mother when she came home.

THE CASE OF THE HURT CAT

Food Suggestion: Each family member chooses one item for a meal. For example, the father chooses the drink, the daughter chooses a dessert, and so forth.

Action Activity: Play "drop the clothespin," or, with younger children, drop blocks into a box.

Song Time: Include "Amazing Grace."

Interest Item: Draw a large question mark on a sheet of paper.

Listening Preparation Question: What happened to the cat?

Story: "I hate that mean old Mrs. Jasper. I am never going to speak to her again," sobbed Mark.

"Why," asked Eddie, "What did she do to you?"

"She ran over my cat this morning when she backed out of her driveway, and she didn't stop. She just kept on going," said Mark.

"Did she kill the cat?" asked Eddie.

"He's at the animal doctor's place. I think Dad calls the doctor a "vet." Dad said the vet didn't know if he would live or not. We won't know for maybe two or three days."

"Isn't that Mrs. Jasper coming home now?" asked Eddie.

"Yes, and I'm going to take my baseball bat and break out the windows in her car!" said Mark, still crying.

"Oh Mark," cried Mrs. Jasper, running across the yard toward the boys. "I'm so sorry. I didn't know that your cat was under my car, and I didn't even feel anything when I ran over him. How is he?"

Mark looked up at Mrs. Jasper. Tears were running down her cheeks. He didn't know what to think. He still wanted to hate her for hurting his cat. But she seemed so sorry.

"We don't know. He is still at the vet's," he whispered. A big lump filled Mark's throat.

"I hope you will forgive me, Mark. I didn't mean to hurt your cat. I was in a hurry and was careless as well. I'm sorry. Can you forgive me?"

Story Question: Three possible ways this story could end are given. Choose the ending that seems best to fit the story. Discuss why you chose the ending. Why did you not choose the other endings?

1. Mark said, "If my cat lives, I'll forgive you, Mrs. Jasper."

2. Mark said, "Yes, I'll forgive you," but in his mind he knew that someday he would get even.

3. Mark realized that everyone, even grown-ups, make mistakes, so he said, "Yes, Mrs. Jasper, I'll forgive you." And he really meant it.

Scripture Passage: "And forgive us our debts, as we forgive our debtors" (Matt. 6:12).

Scripture Question: How would this verse help Mark to forgive Mrs. Jasper?

Scripture Comment for Parents: This familiar verse is part of the Lord's Prayer, also called the Model Prayer. When Jesus told his disciples how to pray, he encouraged them to ask God's forgiveness for their sins. At the same time, he implied that God's willingness to forgive should be our example for dealing with persons who have wronged us. God always is ready to forgive us when we truly are sorry. Likewise, we should be equally willing to forgive.

Prayer Suggestion: Repeat the Lord's Prayer.

Follow-up Activity: For several days keep a list of family accidents such as spilled milk, broken toys, or water left running. Have all such incidents been forgiven? If not, you may wish to spend further time in study of forgiveness.

THE MAGIC TRICK

Food Suggestion: Raid the refrigerator.

Action Activity: If you know any magic tricks, perform them. Frequently the Sunday comics section of the newspaper has magic tricks your children can perform.

Song Time: Include "What a Friend We Have in Jesus."

Interest Item: A nickel.

Listening Preparation Question: Was Mr. Spence really magic?

Story: "Mr. Spence is magic," said Kenny.

"How do you know," asked Larry.

"Because he just got a nickel out of my ear," replied Kenny.

"Maybe he can find me a nickel," said Larry. "Come on. Let's go find him."

"Not now, but after Sunday School I'll ask him," replied Kenny.

The boys ran into their Sunday School room as Mrs. King started to tell the Bible story. "Boys and girls, our story for today is about Jesus healing the crippled man who was lowered down through the roof of a house," said Mrs. King.

"I wonder how Jesus healed him?" whispered Kenny to Larry.

"It must have been magic," replied Larry.

"The crippled man had been sick for a number of years. He had no hope of ever being better," said Mrs. King. "His friends heard of Jesus who could heal people, and they brought the crippled man to him. Because of the crowd, they could not get their friend into the house where Jesus was. They took part of the roof up and lowered the man through the opening. Jesus healed the man, who then picked up his mat and walked away."

Kenny couldn't wait for Mrs. King to finish the story. "Was Jesus magic?" he asked.

Mrs. King smiled. She had seen Mr. Spence and Kenny in the hall. "No, Jesus isn't magic. Jesus is God's Son. He has power over all the universe," she said. "When someone does a magic trick, boys and girls, it is just that—a trick. They have practiced the trick to make you think that you see something that is different from what is really happening. Mr. Spence had that nickel hidden in his hand before he saw you, Kenny," she explained. "He just pretended that he got it from your ear."

"God doesn't trick us," said Larry.

"No, God's power is so strong and his love for us so great that he does not trick us." said Mrs. King.

"Magic is fun to watch and even more fun to learn," she continued. "But no one has magic powers. They just have practiced hard to learn those tricks."

"Would it be all right if I asked Mr. Spence to get a nickel out of my ear?" asked Larry.

"Of course, Larry, but just remember that magic is for fun—not for real."

Story Questions: Why did Kenny think that Mr. Spence was magic? What was the Sunday School story about? Why did Kenny ask if Jesus was magic? How did Mr. Spence do the magic trick? Does God play tricks on us?

Scripture Passage: "And they were all amazed, and they

glorified God, and were filled with fear, saying, we have seen strange things to-day" (Luke 5:26).

Scripture Question: Why were the people afraid?

Scripture Comment for Parents: When we see someone perform a magic trick, we know that they really do not have magic powers. The people who saw Jesus heal the sick man knew that what he had done was no trick. They knew that the sick man had been ill for a long time. And since this was not a trick, the only other explanation was that Jesus had special powers. They did not understand those powers and were afraid of them. Yet, they did give thanks to God for what had been done for the sick man.

Prayer Suggestion: Pray for one or two sick persons you know. Ask that God heal them.

Follow-up Activity: Watch a magic show on television or in person. Discuss the tricks performed. Try to figure out possible ways the magician performed his tricks.

THE BIRTHDAY WISH

Food Suggestion: Cake and ice cream.

Action Activity: Play "Shoot out the Candle." Place a lighted candle on a table. Take turns trying to shoot it out with a water pistol. Make allowances for the ages of children.

Song Time: Include singing "Happy Birthday."

Interest Item: A package of birthday wrapping paper.

Listening Preparation Question: What was Norman's birthday surprise?

Story: Norman and Todd were good friends. They were such good friends that they did just about everything together. When it was nearly time for Norman's birthday, his mother told him that he would not have a birthday party with a lot of friends. Instead he would have a surprise day, and Todd could share it with him.

On Norman's birthday, his mother brought out a beautiful white cake that had a clown decoration on top. "Blow out all the candles," said Todd excitedly, "and your wish will come true."

"What do you mean?" asked Norman.

"Oh, you know," said Todd, "if you make a wish and then blow out all of your candles with one blow, your wish will come true."

"Is that true, Mom?" asked Norman.

"A lot of people like to think so," said his mother.

So Norman closed his eyes, thought hard for a few minutes, and then blew as hard as he could.

"Hurrah!" said Todd, "you blew out all the candles. Now your wish will come true. Tell us what it was."

"I wished we could go someplace special." said Norman.

"This is one time when you will get your wish," said Norman's mother. "The surprise planned for today is that your father will take you and Todd to the amusement park, and you can spend the rest of the day there."

The following Sunday Norman and Todd told their Sunday School teacher about all the fun they had at the amusement park. The teacher, Mr. Flowers, laughed with the boys, and then asked them to take their seats.

"Today's story," said Mr. Flowers, "is about people in the Bible who prayed a lot. Can you name some of the famous people who prayed?"

"I know," said Shane waving his hand to get Mr. Flowers' attention. "Daniel prayed to get out of the lions' den."

"And Jesus prayed before he was killed by the Romans," volunteered Marie.

Norman and Todd raised their hands at the same time, and they both had the same question. "Mr. Flowers, is praying like making a wish?"

"Not really," said Mr. Flowers, "but I can see why you might think both are the same thing. When you make a wish, you are just hoping you'll get something you want for yourself. When you pray, you actually are talking with God."

"But I don't see God when I pray," said Norman.

"No," replied Mr. Flowers, "but God hears you, and he is interested in what you pray. Praying is more than asking a special favor. Praying is telling God thanks for all that he has given you, and it is asking God to help you to live a good life."

"Can't you ask God for anything?" inquired Todd.

"Oh yes," said Mr. Flowers, "God wants us to ask for things we really need, not just toys. And he likes for us to pray for other people."

"Mr. Flowers, does God always answer our prayers?" asked Norman.

"That's a good question," said Mr. Flowers. "God does hear and answer our prayers, but not always in the way we expect. He answers in ways best for us, even if at the time we don't realize what is the best."

"I don't understand," said Norman.

"Look at it this way," said Mr. Flowers. "You had wanted a birthday party, but your parents knew that you would enjoy going to the amusement park more than having a party."

"Now I see," said Norman. "Praying is really a way of telling God that we trust him to take care of us."

"I think that you do understand," said Mr. Flowers. "Now let's talk about Bible people who prayed."

Story Questions: What did Norman want to happen on his birthday? Did he get what he wanted? Why did Todd tell him to make a wish when Norman blew out his birthday candles? Would he have gotten his wish even if he hadn't blown out the candles? What was the Sunday School story about? Is praying like making a wish? What is praying? What should we talk about when we pray? How does God answer our prayers?

Scripture Passage: "After this manner therefore pray ye: Our Father which art in heaven, Hallowed be thy name. Thy kingdom come. Thy will be done in earth, as it is in heaven. Give us this day our daily bread. And forgive us our debts, as we forgive our debtors. And lead us not into temptation, but deliver us from evil: For thine is the kingdom, and the power, and the glory, for ever. Amen." (Matt. 6:9-13).

Scripture Question: What are some of the things asked for in this prayer?

Scripture Comment for Parents: The familiar Lord's Prayer was given by Jesus as a pattern for praying. The first part of the prayer acknowledges the holiness of God and asks that his will be done. Only after words of praise to God does the prayer turn to the personal needs which are food, forgiveness, and guidance.

Prayer Suggestion: Memorize and pray the Lord's Prayer.

Follow-up Activity: Make a prayer calendar for one week, listing different people for whom to pray each day.

TRAFFIC LIGHTS

Food Suggestion: Ask children to plan menu. If possible, allow them to prepare and serve the meal.

Action Activity: Play "Red Light." Leader stands on one side of the room. Others line up on opposite wall. Leader closes his eyes, counts to five, says "Red Light," and opens his eyes. Others are moving toward leader. Anyone caught still advancing must go back to the start of line. Player who reaches leader first is the winner.

Song Time: Sing a song of obedience, such as "Footsteps of Jesus."

Interest Item: Bible open to Ten Commandments.

Listening Preparation Question: Why do we have traffic lights?

Story: "The light is green now, Daddy," said Doug.

"Oh, thanks, Son. I was looking at that new building going up across the street and not watching the traffic light," said Dad.

"Why do we have traffic lights, Daddy?" asked Doug.

"To keep the traffic moving smoothly and to prevent accidents," replied Daddy.

"What would happen if you didn't stop for a red light or a stop sign?" asked Doug.

"Any one of three things would happen, Doug" replied his father. "It is possible that nothing would happen. If no one was coming the other way, or if the other drivers were watching, you might make it through the red light once or even several times."

"Mom and I almost ran a red light once," said Doug, "but we didn't mean to. It just changed to red fast."

"That happens sometimes," said Daddy. "We may not mean to break a law, but if a car were coming the other way, we still could have an accident."

"Is that the second thing that could happen?" asked the boy.

"Yes, Doug, and the third thing is that a policeman just might stop you and remind you of the traffic laws. He might even give you a ticket, and you would have to pay a fine."

"That's mean," said Doug.

"No, the policeman doesn't make the laws, he just tries to make certain that we obey them. It would be very dangerous if everyone just drove anyway they felt like driving."

"Is that why we have laws?" asked Doug.

"Yes, Son, laws are not meant to be punishment. They are to help us have happier, safer lives."

Just then they drove by a church. "Say, Daddy, what about God's laws? What is the purpose for them?"

"Let's use God's Ten Commandments as an example," said the father. "Those Commandments are sort of like traffic lights. Some of the Commandments tell you what you shouldn't do, and others tell you what you should do."

"Oh I see," replied Doug. "They tell you when to stop and when to go."

"Right," laughed Daddy, "and you'll have a happier life if you obey the Commandments."

"But what if you break God's laws? Will he punish you?" inquired Doug.

"Let's remember that God didn't give us laws as punishment.

He gave us laws, or Commandments, so that we would know how to live life at its best. After all, God made us so he should know what is best for us. If we choose to break his laws, what happens afterwards may seem like punishment. Actually, it's God's way of letting us know that we can be happy only if we obey his laws."

Story Questions: Name three things which might happen if you ran a red light? Why do we have laws? How are the Ten Commandments like traffic lights? Why did God give us laws or Commandments? What happens if we break God's laws? What happens if we obey God's laws?

Scripture Passage: "And Moses called all Israel, and said unto them, Hear, O Israel, the statutes and judgments which I speak in your ears this day, that ye may learn them, and keep, and do them" (Deut. 5:1).

Scripture Question: Why did Moses call the people of Israel together?

Scripture Comments for Parents: This verse describes Moses' introduction to the Ten Commandments according to the book of Deuteronomy. Another listing of the Commandments is in Exodus 20. Moses stressed that not only were God's laws to be learned but they were to be obeyed.

Prayer Suggestion: Give thanks to God for people who make laws and for judges and policemen who help enforce the laws. Give thanks for churches which teach us God's laws.

Follow-up Activity: During the week as you are driving with your child, call attention to traffic signs. If the child is old enough, let him do some "backseat" driving, telling you when to stop, go, how fast, and so forth. You might also remember that your child is taking driving lessons from you long before he is old enough to drive.

GOING TO BIG CHURCH

Food Suggestion: Children's choice.
Action Activity: Play hide-and-seek.

Song Time: Include songs you would sing in Sunday worship service.

Interest Center: A Sunday bulletin, church letter, or some other item from your church.

Listening Preparation Question: Listen for at least one reason Tricia liked going to big church.

Story: "Just tell your mother you are going to sit with me, and she'll never know that you weren't in big church," said Beth to Tricia. "Then we can sneak back to our Sunday School room and play while big church is going on."

"But that would be telling a lie," said Tricia, "and besides, I want to go to big church."

"Oh, you know that big church is no fun," said Beth. "Big church is just for big people. It's too boring for kids. We can have a lot more fun playing."

"Big church is so for kids. And you would like it better if you paid more attention to what goes on," replied Tricia.

"All that goes on is the preacher talking, and most of the time I don't understand what he's talking about," said Beth.

"I don't always understand what is said either, but I still like big church," said Tricia, impatiently.

Beth looked around to see if there were any other kids she could get to stay out of big church with her, but all of the other children had already gone. She certainly didn't want to stay in the Sunday School room by herself.

"All right, Tricia," she said, "this Sunday I'll go sit with you in big church, and you can show me what is so special about it."

Beth and Tricia hurried to the door of the sanctuary. At the door they were greeted by a tall usher who leaned forward and said, "Good morning, ladies," as he handed each of the girls a church bulletin.

Tricia turned to Beth and said, "That's one thing I like about big church. They treat everybody like big people." Beth just shrugged her shoulders, but she had never paid much attention before to adults speaking to her in church. On their way to their seat, two other adults stopped them and told them how nice they looked.

Tricia led Beth to a seat near the front of the church. "Why are you sitting so close to the front?" asked Beth.

"So I can see," said Tricia. "You really can't tell what is going on if you sit further back behind all the adults."

Just then the organist started playing a hymn. Tricia leaned over to Beth and whispered, "Another thing I like about big church is the music." The deep tones of the organ seemed to fill the sanctuary with a special feeling.

Then the music director led the congregation in singing several songs. Beth told herself she'd never admit it to Tricia, but she did enjoy singing as loud as she could with the congregation.

Then came time for the offering. The pastor prayed that God would use the money given to help teach boys and girls around the world about Christ. Beth had a new sense of pride as she put her quarter into the offering plate. She realized that there was a real purpose for giving an offering.

When the pastor got up to speak, Beth whispered to Tricia, "Here comes the boring part. What do you do now?"

Tricia whispered back as quickly and quietly as she could. "Listen for the stories. They are always good. When you don't understand what he's talking about, look around for all the things that point to God."

It only took Beth a few minutes to see what Tricia meant about things pointing to God. The colored glass windows were curved to a point on top which made them seem to point upward. There was a cross carved into the pulpit, and that certainly pointed to God. Even the open Bible on the table in front of the pulpit reminded her of God.

But Beth didn't spend much time looking around, because the pastor was speaking about the importance of the church. He said that all the people who made up the church were to continue Christ's work on earth. Then he talked about all the things Christ had done and how the church was to continue that work. Beth thought of the many miracles Christ did, the healing that he did, and all the teaching that he did. And big church became exciting for her.

When the minister of music announced the closing hymn, Beth was surprised that big church was over so soon. She was already looking forward to the next service.

Story Questions: Why did Beth not like big church? What happened when the girls entered the sanctuary? Why did Tricia want to sit near the front? Why did the church take an offering? What did Tricia tell Beth about listening to sermons? What did the pastor say about the church?

Scripture Passage: "And they . . . [continued] daily with one accord in the temple . . . , praising God, and having favour with all the people. And the Lord added to the church daily such as should be saved" (Acts 2:46-47).

Scripture Question: What was being added to the church daily?

Scripture Comment for Parents: This partial description of an early church illustrates what a church should be like. This particular church was enthusiastic, and the enthusiasm spread to others.

Prayer Suggestion: Thank God for your church, and ask God to help your church minister to more people.

Follow-up Activity: Try Tricia's methods of enjoying worship services next Sunday.

How Did God Get Born?

Food Suggestion: Plan something you usually eat only at grandparents' house.

Action Activity: Jump rope. For younger children hold rope on the floor and zigzag it across the floor. Let them try to jump across without touching the rope.

Song Time: Include songs about creation. Use the topical index in hymnal.

Interest Item: Globe or world map.

Listening Preparation Question: Why did Ben's dad have to think a while before answering Ben's question?

Story: "And that's the story of how God created the world," said Dad, closing the Bible.

"I sure wish I could have seen it all taking place," said Ben.

"It must have been a beautiful sight," joined in Mother. "Imagine it being totally dark, and then comes the light shattering the darkness."

"I wish someone had had a television camera there," said Ben.

"That would have been nice," laughed Dad, "but right now its time for you to get ready for bed. I'll bring a glass of water to your room in just a few minutes."

"There's just one thing I don't understand, Dad," said Ben, as he was climbing into bed.

"What's that?" asked Dad.

"I can see how God made the world," said Ben, "but how did God get born?"

"Wow!" said Dad, "that's a tough question, but a good one. I'll have to think about it for a few minutes."

"That's OK, Dad, I'll wait," said Ben, who sat cross-legged in bed with his elbows on his knees and his hands on his chin.

In a moment Dad said, "Ben, the best answer I can give you is that God was never born. He just always has been."

"You mean he didn't have a mother and a father?" said Ben.

"No," responded Dad, "He always existed—even before there were any fathers and mothers."

"What do you mean he always existed?" asked Ben.

Dad thought again for a minute and then said, "You like for me to tell you stories of things I did when I was a little boy—long before you were born."

"Oh, yes," said Ben, "I like to hear about the old days."

Dad laughed as he continued, "And when I was a little boy, I liked to hear stories about things my dad did before I was born."

"Did your father's dad tell stories like that too?" asked Ben.

"Yes," replied Dad, "and if we could know about all the stories that all our grandparents told long, long ago, some of those stories would be about God, because God is older than anyone's grandparent."

"If God is *that* old," quipped Ben, "why doesn't he die?"

"That's another way that God is different," said Dad. "He will never die. God can't get sick or be hurt. Nothing can happen to God to make him die. He will always live."

"That makes me feel kinda good inside," said Ben, as he snuggled beneath the covers.

"How's that?" asked Dad as he turned out the lights.

"Now I know that no matter how old I get to be," said Ben, "I'll always have God with me."

Story Questions: What story had Ben's dad read to him? What book was he reading? What did Ben's dad say about God being born? How old is God? Why did Ben say that he felt good inside?

Scripture Passage: "Before the mountains were brought forth, or ever thou hadst formed the earth and the world, even from everlasting to everlasting, thou art God" (Ps. 90:2).

Scripture Question: Which is older, God or the mountains?

Scripture Comment for Parents: The writer of this psalm beautifully expressed the same truth illustrated in the story. God has been, is, and will be present in every generation.

Prayer Suggestion: Ask God to help you to remember that he is always with you.

Follow-up Activity: Go on a rock hunt. Find a book or encyclopedia to tell you characteristics of types of rock and how old they are. Remind children of the story and that God was before the creation of the world.

HOW DO YOU SEE JESUS?

Food Suggestion: Pancakes. Make faces by adding raisins for eyes, half of a pineapple slice for a mouth, and a pat of butter for the nose.

Action Activity: Play "Statues." Each person jumps, swings his arms, and makes faces until the leader calls, "Freeze." The leader then tells each person what they remind him of: monkey, queen, clown, etc. Another person becomes the leader and the game continues.

Song Time: Include "Let Others See Jesus in You."

Interest Item: Pictures of your family.

Listening Preparation Question: Where did Dan have a picture of Jesus?

Story: Dan and Diana stood impatiently in the photographer's waiting room while their mother ran a comb through their hair one more time.

"This shirt is hot and my pants are itchy," said Dan.

"I don't like to wear a dress on Saturday," grumbled Diana.

"Now hush!" implored Mother. "This was the only time I could make an appointment to have your picture taken in time to get it back for your grandmother's birthday."

"My, my, don't you all look nice," said the photographer. "Come on in and let's see how you look through the camera."

"I remember you," said Dan, "You have taken my picture before."

"I sure did, Dan. You have really grown since you were here the last time," said the photographer.

"That's why Mom wants our picture taken," said Diana. "She said Grandmother won't know us by next summer if we don't send her a photograph."

"Children, sit here on this bench," said the photographer. "Dan, you sit behind Diana. Hold your head to the left, Dan. Good! Diana, try not to squint your eyes. The lights won't hurt. That's fine!" *Click* went the camera. "Move a little closer to Dan, Diana." *Click.*

"OK, now let's have Dan stand behind you, Diana. Fine!" *Click.* "One more and I think we are finished," said the photographer. *Click.* "That's all children, tell your mother to come back next Friday for the proofs."

"Thank-you," said the children, skipping out of the studio.

"You two look happier than when you went in," said Mother.

"He was nice," said Dan. "He remembered taking my picture before. Let's go home and let me get off these itchy clothes."

"Mother," said Diana, climbing in the car. "Did they take pictures of people when Jesus was on earth?"

"No, Honey, cameras weren't invented then," replied Mother.

"Then how come I have a picture of Jesus in my Bible?" asked Dan.

"That's just an artist's idea of what Jesus might have looked like, Dan," said Mother smiling.

"I wish they had invented cameras then so we could see a real picture of Jesus," said Diana.

"Do you know the best way to see Jesus, Diana?" asked Mother.

"How?" asked Diana.

"We can't see what Jesus actually looked like," answered Mother. "But we can see his goodness in people who believe and trust in him. His life shines through them."

"I don't understand," said Dan.

"Dan, the photographer who took your picture today is not very good-looking. He is fat and he has very little hair, yet you really didn't pay much attention to those things because he was so kind. You could see Jesus in his life. Do you understand now?" asked Mother.

"I think so," replied Dan. "We really don't need a camera to see Jesus. We can see him in people who love him."

Story Questions: Why did Dan and Diana have their pictures made? Did anyone take a photograph of Jesus when he was on earth? How did Dan get a picture of Jesus in his Bible? What is the best way to see Jesus?

Scripture Passage: "Christ liveth in me: and the life which I now live in the flesh I live by the faith of the Son of God, who loved me, and gave himself for me" (Gal. 2:20).

Scripture Question: How can you show others that Christ lives in you?

Scripture Comment for Parents: When Paul accepted Christ, he felt as if Christ had spiritually moved into his body and that Christ was at the controls of his thoughts, speech, and actions. Therefore, he could proudly claim that the life he *now* lived (as opposed to the way he lived before accepting Christ) was all to the glory of Christ. Any boasting that Paul did was boasting about Christ, not himself.

Prayer Suggestion: Thank God for specific people who live in such a way that they give evidence of Christ in their lives.

Follow-up Activity: Cut pictures from magazines or newspaper of people who are not well-known but who have interesting faces. Discuss these pictures. Make up stories of what you think these people are really like. Even the young children can respond by telling you if a face is happy, sad, or angry.

HOW MUCH DOES CHURCH COST?

Food Suggestion: Decide on a maximum cost for the meal. Let the child (or children) plan the menu, but you help them keep the cost within the budget.

Action Activity: Have a potato race. Give each participant a potato and a tablespoon. Let them run around the room. When the potato falls off the spoon that person is out. The last person to drop his potato is the winner.

Song Time: Include "O Worship the King."

Interest Item: Small basket with a few coins in it.

Listening Preparation Question: How much do you have to pay to attend church?

Story: Kevin watched intently as Carolyn searched through the small white purse she was carrying. Both were seated in children's worship service, and the service was almost to the point where the offering plates were to be passed.

Kevin clutched the coin in his hand while a boy and a girl went to the front of the room to receive the offering plates from Mr. Morgan. Then two children began passing the offering plates to each row of seated children. Reluctantly, Kevin dropped his coin into the plate and then held out the plate for Carolyn to take. Instead, she whispered to Kevin, "Please hold it for me. I can't find my money." Then she held her purse upside down over the offering plate. She shook the purse vigorously. Several coins fell into the plate. When the coins stopped falling, Carolyn gave the purse an extra shake just to make certain every coin had gone into the plate.

After the worship service Kevin said to Carolyn, "Why did you put all your money into the offering plate? You didn't have to pay all that money to get into church."

"I don't have to pay any money to go to church," replied Carolyn. "I gave all my money because I wanted to. Do you think you have to pay to go to church?"

"Of course you do," said Kevin. "You have to pay to do anything. You have to pay to go to the movie or Fair Park. The only difference is that all those other places you have to give your money before you can get in. At church they let you wait until the program has been going on for a while before they take your money."

"Oh, you've got it all wrong!" exclaimed Carol. "You don't pay to go to church. Church is free."

"Oh yeah," growled Kevin loudly, shaking his finger at Carol. "If church is free, how come my parents give me money each Sunday and tell me to be sure and put it into the offering plate? And how come they pass the offering plate each Sunday?"

"OK, OK," said Carol. "Don't be so loud. Listen, when you go to the movie or to Fair Park, they tell you how much you have to pay to get in don't they?"

"Of course they do," sneered Kevin.

"Well, has anyone ever told you how much you had to give at church?" asked Carol.

"No," admitted Kevin.

"And has anyone at church told you if you didn't give that you couldn't stay for the rest of the service?"

"No." Kevin again admitted, weakly.

By now Kevin was really confused. "Why do we give money to church, Carol?" he asked.

"Come with me," said Carol. "I'll show you one reason and then I'll tell you another."

Carol led Kevin down a hallway to a large bulletin board. On the bulletin board was a large drawing of a coin. The coin looked like it had been cut into pieces like a pie. Some of the pieces were very large, and others were very small. Pointing to the drawing Carol said, "This poster shows how our money is used after we put it into the offering plate. Part of it is used to pay for the heat and lights in the building, and one large part is used to help missionaries around the world."

"I think I understand why we give to church, but you said you'd tell me another reason," said Kevin.

"Yes," said Carol, "and this is the best reason of all. Giving to church is one way we show God that we love him. When you think about how much God loves us, you want to give him all you can."

Story Questions: What did Carol do when the offering plate was passed to her? What did Kevin think was the reason for giving money to church? Why did Carol show Kevin the poster of a coin? What did the picture mean? What was Carol's best reason for giving to the church?

Scripture Passage: "Every man according as he purposeth in his heart, so let him give; not grudgingly, or of necessity: for God loveth a cheerful giver" (2 Cor. 9:7).

Scripture Question: Why should a person be cheerful or happy when they give to church?

Scripture Comment for Parents: God wants us to give to church as an expression of gratitude and love for him. Giving should not be a meaningless ritual; it should be a genuine act of worship. Giving part of an income back to God is a way of telling God that we trust him to meet our daily needs.

Prayer Suggestion: Pray that your gifts to church will be used in a special way to honor God.

Follow-up Activity: With the children's help, estimate the cost to the church for providing one year of religious instruction for one child. Include cost of literature, art supplies, parties, and other things.

Character Development

A SCARY SATURDAY

Food Suggestion: Breakfast cereal.

Action Activity: Play "Simon says." This is an old favorite. The leader makes some action or movement which the group follows only if the leader has preceded his action by saying "Simon says." Player who does the action without "Simon says" is out of the game.

Song Time: Include "Onward, Christian Soldiers."

Interest Item: A telephone.

Listening Preparation Question: How did television help Greg and his dad?

Story: "Oh, great," thought Greg, as he opened his eyes. "It's Saturday. I can watch cartoons this morning, and Dad and I are going to the circus tonight. Whoopee!" he yelled as he jumped out of bed.

"I'll have breakfast ready in a minute," called Dad from the kitchen. "Mother and Aunt Jill went shopping."

Greg settled down in front of the television. "Maybe Dad would let me eat breakfast in the family room," he thought. Just then he heard a loud crash which was followed by his Dad making a funny noise.

"Come help me, Greg!" called Dad. Greg ran into the kitchen. "I've cut my arm badly," said Dad. "Get me a towel to hold against the cut."

Greg hurried into the bathroom and got the first clean towel he saw. When he got back to the kitchen, his dad was sitting on the floor. "Now, Greg," he said, "I'm hurt pretty badly. I need the doctor. Can you help me?"

By now Greg was really scared. "I wish Mom were here," he thought. "What am I going to do?" His head was pounding and his throat felt tight. "I've got to help Dad!" "I know," he said aloud. "On television they say dial 911 for emergencies." Greg ran to the phone. The operator took his name and address and told him to open the door for the ambulance men. Then Greg ran back to the kitchen.

"I knew you could handle everything. You are a brave boy," said Greg's father.

Soon the ambulance arrived. "You really are a brave boy," said the ambulance driver. "You did the right thing. Your dad will be fine."

"I'm glad," said Greg, "but there is one thing I don't understand. Both you and Dad said I was brave. How could I be brave? I was so scared until you came."

The man laughed. "Being brave doesn't mean that you aren't afraid, Greg. It means you go ahead and do what you must even if you are very frightened."

Story Questions: Why was Greg's dad preparing breakfast instead of his mother? What did Greg plan to do that day? What happened that was a surprise? What did Greg's dad want him to do? How did Greg feel about his dad being hurt? What did Greg's dad and the ambulance driver say about Greg? How can a person be scared and brave at the same time?

Scripture Passage: "Though I walk through the valley of the shadow of death, I will fear no evil: for thou art with me" (Ps. 23:4).

Scripture Question: Who do you think will be with you even in scary times?

Scripture Comment for Parents: This verse is part of a favorite psalm which tells of God's continual watchcare. Much of the psalm deals with how God leads an individual to have good and satisfying experiences. Often people think God is with them only when they have good experiences, but the writer of this psalm says that God is with him in scary times as well as happy times. The writer declares that he will not be scared even if he is in danger of death because God is with him. We may not be able to keep from being scared sometimes, but we can still be brave because we know that God is with us and will help us.

Prayer Suggestion: Ask God to help you to be brave and to think quickly in times of emergencies.

Follow-up Activity: Make an emergency telephone list. If the child does not know how to read, draw or cut out pictures which illustrate different emergency situations. Teach the child how to dial the operator and ask for help.

Jell-O and Garbage

Food Suggestion: Jell-O dessert.

Action Activity: Play charades, using titles of favorite songs.

Song Time: Sing the songs used in the activity.

Interest Item: A box of Jell-O.

Listening Preparation Question: What good things go in Jell-O?

Story: Scott was crying as he came into the kitchen where his mother was cleaning up after supper.

"Daddy won't let me watch the horror movie," he cried. "I never get to do anything!"

Mother said, "How about helping me make some Jell-O?"

Scott, still unhappy, went to the cabinet and took out a box of lemon Jell-O. He opened the box and poured the dry mixture into a bowl. Mother added boiling water while Scott stirred the fast-dissolving grains.

"Let's pretend your mind is this bowl of Jell-O, Scott," said Mother. Scott giggled. "These marshmallows are all the games you know how to play," she added.

Scott poured in a can of fruit cocktail. "This is all I have learned at school," he said, "and these bananas are all the Bible stories I know."

"Now Scott, pass me those coffee grounds and potato peels," said Mother.

"No," shouted Scott, "I don't want garbage in my Jell-O."

"And your daddy and I don't want garbage in your mind either," Mother replied. "We want to keep your mind clean and healthy. There are fine, healthy things to do and see and there are things that are garbage for our minds."

"I see," laughed Scott. "We don't need garbage in our stomach or in our heads. Both places it can make us sick."

"You are so right, Scott," replied Mother.

Story Questions: What made Scott unhappy? Why did Scott's mother ask Scott to pretend the bowl of Jell-O was his mind? What are some of the things Scott pretended to put into the Jell-O? What was it that Scott did not want in the Jell-O? What did Scott's mother mean when she said she did not want "garbage" in Scott's mind? What are some healthy things for your mind?

Scripture Passage: "And be not conformed to this world, but be ye transformed by the renewing of your mind, that ye may prove what is that good, and acceptable, and perfect will of God" (Rom. 12:2).

Scripture Question: What can you do to show others God's goodness?

Scripture Comment for Parents: There are three difficult but important key words in this verse of Scripture. The first difficult word is *conformed.* It means "to be like something else." Christians are not to be like other people who do not believe in or follow God's teaching. The second word is *transform,* which means that Christians are to be "changed" or different people who follow God's teaching. The final important word is *renewing,* which means "to make new again." We can continually make our minds like new again by putting into our mind those things of which God would approve, such as what the Bible teaches.

Prayer Suggestion: Thank God for good books, songs, and television programs. Ask him to help choose the good things and to leave alone the "garbage" things.

Follow-up Activity: Through the week monitor children's television viewing. Help them decide which programs are healthy for their minds and which are garbage. Also, if you wish, make more Jell-O, allowing children to add extra ingredients.

LORI'S SPELLING TEST

Food Suggestion: Try to make the family feel as special as if they were company. Fix an attractive dish of cheese, fruit, and crackers.

Action Activity: Play "Spear the Raisin." Each player is given a small bowl of raisins and a toothpick. At a given signal each player must stick the raisins one at a time on the toothpick. Player who spears the most raisins wins.

Song Time: Include " 'Tis So Sweet to Trust in Jesus."

Listening Preparation Question: Why did Lori not want to go to school again?

Interest Item: Toy fire truck.

Story: "I wish I didn't have to go home," thought Lori as she climbed on the school bus. All the way home Lori felt more and more miserable.

"Oh, Mother!" cried Lori as she ran in the door.

"What's wrong, Lori? Nothing could be that bad!" said Mother as she looked at her daughter's tear-stained face.

"I did something terrible!" whispered Lori, looking down at the floor.

"Let's sit down and talk about it," said Mother.

"I cheated on my spelling test, and Mrs. Judd caught me," sobbed Lori.

"Why Lori! You know you shouldn't cheat. And you knew your spelling words anyway. Why did you do that?" asked Mother.

"We get a special treat if we don't miss any words for six weeks, and I was afraid I wouldn't get the treat," sobbed Lori. "I am so embarrassed. I don't ever want to go to school again. I must be the worst person in the whole world!"

"Now Lori, you know you shouldn't cheat, and I doubt if you will do it again," said Mother sternly, "but I can understand.

You know that sometimes we all do things of which we are ashamed. We just have to say, 'I'm sorry,' swallow our pride, and go on."

"But Mother! You never did anything bad like cheat, did you?"

"One time I told my teacher that my daddy was a fireman," said Mother.

"But Granddaddy sold cars!" exclaimed Lori.

"I know but I just thought it sounded glamorous to say that my daddy rode on the fire truck and saved people from burning buildings." said Mother.

"Did someone tell on you?" asked Lori.

"No, my teacher called our house and asked daddy if he would speak to the class about fire prevention. That's how they both found out," said Mother smiling.

"Were you punished?" asked Lori.

"Yes, I was. I had to apologize to the class, and I couldn't go out and play for a week," said Mother. "But the worst punishment was what I gave myself," she continued. "I felt so terrible that even after my class, my teacher, and even my daddy forgot about what I had done, I couldn't seem to forgive myself."

"What did you do?" asked Lori.

"I prayed about it, Lori. I asked God to forgive me, and he did. And only then was I able to forgive myself."

"Will God forgive me?" asked Lori.

"Oh, yes!" said Mother. "Do you want to pray?"

Lori prayed: "Dear Lord, I am so sorry I cheated on my spelling test today. Please forgive me. Help me to be strong and not cheat again. And Lord, please help me to forgive myself. Amen."

Story Questions: What had Lori done wrong? How did she feel about it? What did Lori's mother suggest Lori do? Had Lori's mother ever done anything she was ashamed of doing? How was she punished? What did Lori's Mother say was the worst punishment? What did she do to get forgiveness? What did Lori do?

Scripture Passage: "Create in me a clean heart, O God; and renew a right spirit within me" (Ps. 51:10).

Scripture Question: Why would someone feel that they needed a "clean heart"?

Scripture Comments for Parents: When we sin, we feel inwardly stained and polluted. Actually there is nothing we can do to remove that feeling. Only God can remove the burden of sin from our heart. Sin comes from having a wrong, rebellious spirit. Like the psalmist, when we sin, we have to ask God to restore a godly spirit to us. Once we have confessed and committed our sins to him, we need not dwell in grief over our wrongdoing, because God has already forgiven us.

Prayer Suggestion: Pray for forgiveness. Ask God to help you to forgive yourself as well.

Follow-up Activity: Many children seem to feel that they cannot measure up to adult standards and that their parents are perfect. This might be the time for the parents to tell the children about something they did wrong as children. Be sure to tell what were the consequences.

BLAKE'S TEMPER

Food Suggestion: Popcorn, peanuts, or something you would eat at a sporting event.

Action Activity: Shadow box. Arrange a lamp so that shadows can be cast on a wall. Then box or fight your own shadow. You might want to make the activity time like a real boxing match and ring a bell between rounds. Perhaps Dad could be a referee and declare the shadow or the child the winner of the match.

Song Time: Include "All Hail the Power of Jesus' Name."

Interest Item: Draw two faces on a sheet of paper. Make one a happy, smiling face. Make the other with the corners of the mouth pointing downward—indicating unhappiness and anger.

Listening Preparation Question: What did Blake need to practice?

Story: Blake knew that he was in trouble when Mr. Owens, the principal, came into his classroom.

"I bet that Tommy told on me," mumbled Blake under his breath. "I didn't mean to hit him but he just made me so mad!"

Mr. Owens motioned for Blake to follow him to the office. Blake's heart seemed to pound in his chest, his throat hurt, and his hands felt all sweaty.

"Sit down, Blake," said Mr. Owens. "Tommy has made a complaint, and I want to know if it is true."

Blake looked at the floor. "Tattletale," he thought.

"Did you hit Tommy?" asked Mr. Owens.

Blake nodded his head.

"Look at me when I'm talking to you," said Mr. Owens. "Why did you hit Tommy?"

"I guess I was mad because he said he could run faster than I could," answered Blake.

"Can he run faster?" inquired Mr. Owens.

Blake nodded, "Most of the time."

"It sounds to me as if you lost your temper, Blake. You were mad because Tommy is a better runner. Is that true?" asked Mr. Owens.

"I guess so," answered Blake. "Are you going to paddle me?"

"What do you think I should do?" asked the principal.

"I don't like to be paddled," said Blake in a low voice.

Mr. Owens smiled. "I don't imagine Tommy likes to be hit either, do you?

"Blake, you must practice self-control. I want you to apologize to Tommy. I also want you to think about what happened today. Every time you feel that you are losing your temper, I want you to take two deep breaths and say, 'If I lose my temper I'll hurt myself more than anyone else.' I also want you to come back next week and tell me if you have practiced better self-control."

Blake worked hard all week. A couple of times on the playground he got mad. He wanted to hit someone, but instead he did what Mr. Owens told him to do.

Soon a whole week had passed. Mr. Owens saw Blake in the hall. "How's the temper doing?" he asked. "Are you practicing self-control?"

Blake smiled, "I haven't gotten into a fight all week" he said. "But it hasn't been easy."

Mr. Owens laughed. "I didn't say that it would be easy. I'm proud of you. Now keep trying."

Blake stood straight. He felt ten feet tall.

Story Questions: How did Blake know that he was in trouble? Why did he get angry with Tommy? What was Blake afraid that the principal would do? What did the principal tell Blake to do? Was Blake able to control his temper?

Scripture Passage: "There hath no temptation taken you but such as is common to man: but God is faithful, who will not suffer you to be tempted above that ye are able; but will with the temptation also make a way to escape, that ye may be able to bear it" (1 Cor. 10:13).

Scripture Question: What has God promised to do whenever we are tempted to lose our temper or do something wrong?

Scripture Comments for Parents: All temptations are personal, yet this verse tells us that no temptation is so unique that we cannot overcome it. Others have and still do face the same temptations. We cannot justify yielding to temptation by saying that our situation is unique or special. The Scriptures emphatically state that God always will provide a way for us to escape temptation. Whether or not to take the way of escape is our decision.

Prayer Suggestion: Pray for strength to resist temptation and to follow God's way.

Follow-up Activity: Have a pretend argument and practice Mr. Owen's suggestions on how not to lose your temper. Take turns.

Two Arrows

Food Suggestion: Hot dogs.

Action Activity: Play darts. If a dart board is not available use three boxes of graduated size. Place one inside the other and give each box a point value. Place them on the floor several feet from the player. Players have three turns to throw a small ball into the boxes. Player with highest score wins.

Song Time: Include "This Is My Father's World."

Interest Item: An arrow if one is available. Or use the dart board.

Listening Preparation Question: What did Eddie do to his arrow?

Story: "OK boys, let's load into the van," called Mr. Vance. Mr. Vance was the counselor for a boys group at church, and he was taking his group to the park for a hike and a weiner roast. All the boys liked Mr. Vance. He could tell stories like no one else they knew. Sometimes his stories were very serious, but most of the time his stories were so funny that the boys would laugh and laugh.

Mr. Vance could sing, too, so he and the boys sang loudly all the way from the church parking lot to the park. "Here we are!" yelled all the boys as they piled out of the van at the park. "Let's start our hike."

"Wait just a minute," said Mr. Vance loudly. "I need to tell you about the trail we'll follow today. I want you to be on the lookout for arrows."

"Did Indians used to live here?" asked Charles, really wondering if Indians were in the park right then.

"Indians probably lived here a long, long time ago, but it is not Indian arrows that you may find. Part of the trail we take crosses the old archery range. You might find one or two arrows that someone has left."

"All right," yelled the boys enthusiastically, as they moved off down the trail.

Not too much later another yell echoed through the trees.

"I've found one, Mr. Vance!" shouted Eddie, as he waved a long arrow with bright orange feathers and a steel-pointed tip. Just then Carl spotted another arrow lodged in a bush. However, Carl's arrow just had a steel tip, but no feathers. The feathers had been stripped from the arrow as it had dropped through the branches of the bush. Still, Carl was happy to have found an arrow.

No one else found any arrows, so the hike continued. Eventually the boys reached the end of the trail and headed back to the van. Every one looked for arrows again when they crossed the archery range for the second time, but there were no more to be found. Eddie waved his arrow around a lot and bragged about how his arrow was so much better and prettier than Carl's.

Once they returned to the van, Mr. Vance told the boys to gather wood for building the fire. Soon there was a roaring fire going, and they were ready to roast their weiners.

"Say, what's the sad look all about?" Mr. Vance inquired of Eddie. "You were all smiles with that arrow of yours a few minutes ago." Eddie didn't say anything, he just held up the arrow for Mr. Vance to see. "Why part of the fiberglass stem has been burnt, and it is melted!" exclaimed Mr. Vance. Eddie then explained that he decided to stir up the fire with his long arrow, but when he placed the tip in the fire, the arrow stem melted. Now his arrow was burnt black and misshapened. Carl's arrow without the feathers looked better than Eddie's.

Later that evening as the boys sat around the fire, Mr. Vance told a story about the two arrows. He pointed out that Eddie's arrow had once been beautiful and much nicer than Carl's, but Eddie's arrow had not been taken care of, so now Carl's arrow was the nicer one. Mr. Vance concluded by saying, "God has given to each of you special abilities. You can use those abilities to honor God, or you can use the abilities in ways that displease God. Or you can choose not to use the abilities at all. Each of you will make one of those three choices. Let's pray that everyone here will make the right choice.

Story Questions: What did Mr. Vance tell the boys to look for? Did the boys find Indian arrows? What was the difference between Eddie's and Carl's arrows? What caused Carl's arrow to become the best one? What did Mr. Vance say about using your abilities?

Scripture Passage: "Neither yield you your members as instruments of unrighteousness unto sin: but yield yourselves unto God, as those that are alive from the dead, and your members as instruments of righteousness unto God" (Rom. 6:13).

Scripture Question: Substitute the word *abilities* for the word *members* in this verse. What does the verse urge you to do?

Scripture Comment for Parents: Each ability we have can be a means of living sinfully, or a means of living for God. Only as we give ourselves completely in faith and commitment to God will our abilities become "instruments of righteousness unto God."

Prayer Suggestion: Pray that God will make you aware of ways to use your abilities to honor him.

Follow-up Activity: Show children two Styrofoam cups. Place one in the oven at 350° for a few minutes. Take the melted cup out of the oven and compare the two cups. Apply the story of the arrows to the cups.

Special Concerns

DOES IT HURT TO DIE?

(Caution: The following true story should not be read at night or when the child is upset. This story could be used when there has been a death, or when a question about death has been raised. We do strongly suggest that you make a special time to use this story and to discuss death with the family before a time of crisis).

Food Suggestion: Family favorite.

Action Activity: Family backrub. Sit on floor according to age, one in front of other, and rub each other's back.

Song Time: Sing songs of joy in future life such as "When We All Get to Heaven."

Interest Item: Fresh flower.

Listening Preparation Question: Why did the children cry?

Story: Donna sat very still. She could not believe what she was hearing. The principal was standing in front of her classroom. She was saying that Mrs. Allen, Donna's teacher, was dead.

Just yesterday Mrs. Allen was right here in this room, and now she was gone.

Mrs. Craighead, the principal, told the class that Mrs. Allen was in a car accident and had been killed instantly.

Some of the children started to cry. Mrs. Craighead said that it was all right to cry. She said it was all right to feel sad, and that they all would miss Mrs. Allen very much. Then Mrs. Craighead asked if anyone had a question.

Slowly Donna raised her hand.

"Yes, Donna," said Mrs. Craighead.

"Does it hurt to die?" Donna asked.

"Sometimes during sickness or an injury our bodies will feel pain," said Mrs. Craighead, "but death does not always mean pain. Let me explain it this way. You know how sometimes you are afraid, or you don't feel well and you go lie down on your parent's bed and go to sleep. And then the next morning you find yourself in your own bed. Sometime during the night your father moved you back to your own room. I think that must be how dying feels. We are in one place, and then we are with Jesus. He comes and takes us home with him. It won't be sad or it won't hurt. We will be in heaven."

"We shouldn't feel sorry for Mrs. Allen," continued Mrs. Craighead. "She is in heaven with Jesus. We will miss her here, but soon we will be able to remember just the happy times we had together. Then we won't feel so sad. We will be able to thank God that she was here with us for a while."

Story Questions: What had happened to Mrs. Allen? Why did the school principal say that it was all right to cry? How did the principal answer the question, Does it hurt to die? What would the children be able to remember?

Scripture Passage: "Yea, though I walk through the valley of the shadow of death, I will fear no evil: for thou art with me; thy rod and thy staff they comfort me" (Ps. 23:4).

Scripture Comment for Parents: This verse from the favorite twenty-third Psalm was written from the viewpoint of a shepherd. Often the ancient shepherd would have to lead his flock down a pathway through crevices and along other places which had many deep dark shadows. Because of the intense sunlight, the contrasting dark shadows made it impossible to see if a lion or some other wild animal was hidden in a shadow, ready to attack. The rod and staff were shepherds' standard equipment used to guide and protect the sheep. God's guiding presence in our life even at a time of death will be a comfort to us.

Prayer Suggestion: Pray for the family of someone you know who has died recently.

Follow-up Activity: Visit a funeral home at a time when few visitors would be present.

LOVE DIVIDED

Food Suggestion: Honor one person with their favorite food.

Action Activity: Play a favorite family table game.

Song Time: Include "Blest Be the Tie."

Interest Item: Picture of a family.

Listening Preparation Question: What made Billy and his parents sad?

Story: "Daddy, what is divorce?" asked Peggy.

"Why do you ask?" said Daddy.

"Well," said Peggy, "Aunt Sue and Billy come to see us, but Uncle Bob doesn't come any more. I asked Billy and he said it's because they are divorced."

"Divorce means that a husband and wife are no longer married, Peggy."

"But why?" said Peggy.

"There are many reasons for divorce, Peggy. We are always sorry to see a marriage end. But sometimes it happens."

"Are you and Mommy going to get a divorce?" inquired Peggy.

"No, Peggy, we aren't," said Daddy, giving her a hug.

Peggy, still disturbed, asked, "Does this mean that Uncle Bob doesn't love Billy anymore?"

"No, Peggy. The feelings Uncle Bob has for Billy are still the same. But it does mean that he doesn't see him as often. Now Billy will spend some weekends and part of the summer with his dad."

"Do divorced kids always live with their mothers?" asked Peggy.

"No," said Dad, "sometimes the judge decides that the child or children will live with their fathers or even someone else. And, Peggy, the child whose parents are divorced is not divorced. He still loves both parents, even though he lives most of the time with one or the other."

"I know why Uncle Bob and Aunt Sue got a divorce," said Peggy. "I bet it is because Billy broke that window and got into trouble."

"No, Peggy, remember the problems in a divorce are between a husband and wife. Sometimes children feel that they are to blame, but that isn't true. Don't blame Billy for his parents' problems. And remember, it is a sad time for all of them."

"When I grow up I'm not going to get divorced," said Peggy.

"I hope not," said Dad. "You know that your mother and I are already praying for the person you may someday marry, and we are praying for your future happiness."

Story Questions: What is divorce? What was Peggy afraid would happen to her parents? Does Billy's dad still love him? Did Billy do anything to cause the divorce? Why were Peggy's parents praying for whoever Peggy would marry? Do you know anyone who is divorced? How does this story make you feel?

Scripture Passage: "Nevertheless let everyone of you in particular so love his wife as himself; and the wife see that she reverence her husband" (Eph. 5:33).

Scripture Question: How much love should a person have for the person to whom they are married?

Scripture Comment for Parents: This verse summarizes the teaching of several preceding verses which deal with the husband and wife relationship. The apostle Paul, who wrote the verse, used the relationship between Christ and his church as a model for the husband and wife relationship. A husband and wife are to be devoted totally to one another. Their loyalty should be to each other above all else. They should be so devoted to one another that they become like one person instead of two. In other words, they should become so mutually dependent upon one another, so full of respect for each other, so concerned about the well-being of each other, so much in love, that to other people they seem to be one person.

Prayer Suggestion: Thank God for leading the parents to love and marry each other. Ask God to help the child be ready for marriage when the time comes and to seek God's guidance in choosing a mate. Pray for that future mate.

Follow-up Activity: Cut out family pictures from magazines. Use the pictures to act out family situations.

A NEW CHURCH

Food Suggestion: Fix a familiar food in a different way. For example, make banana boats. Cut a lengthwise split in an unpeeled banana. Stuff with chocolate bits and marshmallows. Wrap in foil and heat until chocolate and marshmallows are semi-melted.

Action Activity: Duck walk. Each person stoops down and holds ankles with hands. Winner is the person who walks the farthest without falling.

Song Time: Ask children to sing songs they have learned in Sunday School.

Interest Item: Picture of your church, possibly taken from a church bulletin.

Listening Preparation Question: What was the first thing that helped Carolyn to begin liking her new church?

Story: "I don't want to go to a new church," said Carolyn as she got out of the car.

"Now come on," said Mother. "You know our old church is too far away since we moved."

Carolyn stood and looked all around her. Everything was different. This modern stone and glass building didn't look like a church in her opinion. A church should have big white columns and be made of red brick. This church didn't even have a steeple.

Inside, Carolyn saw no one she knew. At her old church she and her friends all would walk to Sunday School together. Here she didn't even know where to go.

"This must be your class," said Daddy. "We'll meet you here right after Sunday School."

Now Carolyn was really frightened. How she missed Mrs. Edwards and all her old friends. She didn't want to go into this new room. Tears began to well up in Carolyn's eyes. "I want to go home," she thought.

Just then the door opened. "Why," thought Carolyn, "they have the same pictures on the bulletin board as we had at my old church." "Come in," said a lady in a blue dress. "My name is Mrs. Anderson. Would you like to join us this morning?"

Carolyn walked through the door. A girl playing the Autoharp looked at her and smiled. "Maybe this new church isn't so bad," thought Carolyn. "It doesn't look like my other church, and none of my old friends are here, but I think it feels like a good place to be."

Story Questions: Why did Carolyn have to go to a new church? How did she think a church should look? What did she miss about her old church? Name three things that helped her decide that the new church felt like a good place to be.

Scripture Passage: "I was glad when they said unto me, Let us go into the house of the Lord" (Ps. 122:1).

Scripture Question: What is "the house of the Lord"?

Scripture Comment for Parents: An invitation to attend church, or even an announcement that it is time to go to church, should cause each person to be filled with joyful anticipation. A church is not just a building. A church is a group of Christians gathered together for learning, singing, inspiration, and worship.

Prayer Suggestion: Pray for your pastor and Sunday School teacher. Ask God to help them as they teach and preach.

Follow-up Activity: While riding in the car, point out different types of church buildings. Discuss what is a church.

WHEN VIRGINIA WENT TO THE HOSPITAL

Food Suggestion: Prepare some nonspillable food. Eat on trays in a bedroom. If you do not have enough trays, cookie sheets will work well.

Action Activity: Play "Gossip." Sit in a circle on the floor. Leader whispers a phrase or a sentence to the person on the right, who in turn whispers the same thing to the next person. Continue around the circle until returning to the leader who tells what was reported to him and also what he had said originally. The game can be played with as few as three people.

Song Time: Include "There Is a Name I Love to Hear."

Interest Item: Something from a hospital. Possibly an old hospital identification bracelet.

Listening Preparation Question: What is a chaplain?

Story: "Mrs. Sowell," said the school nurse on the phone, "I think you'd better take Virginia to the doctor. She is lying down in the school clinic now, and she says she doesn't feel well at all."

Mrs. Sowell quickly called Dr. Rider, the pediatrician, to see if she could take Virginia straight to the doctor's office.

Then she drove to Virginia's school. "I feel horrible!" Virginia said as her mother entered the school clinic, "and my stomach hurts."

As soon as they arrived at Dr. Rider's office, the nurse took them to an examining room. In just a few minutes Dr. Rider was feeling of Virginia's stomach and asking about her pain. Then he said, "Virginia, I think you have a 'hot tummy,' and I want you to be examined by a surgeon."

"What," asked Mrs. Sowell, "is a hot tummy?"

Dr. Rider laughed. "That's what we call a case of appendicitis. The surgeon will have to make the final diagnosis, and he can operate if need be."

Upon hearing the word *operate,* Virginia perked up. She was a little scared and excited at the same time. She had never been operated on before.

Dr. Crow, the surgeon, agreed that Virginia needed to have her appendix removed. He called the hospital and scheduled the operation for later that afternoon. Dr. Crow told Mrs. Sowell to take Virginia right on to the hospital. She didn't even have time to go home and get a pair of pajamas. The doctor assured Virginia that the hospital would provide a gown for her.

Mr. Sowell was waiting at the admissions office when Virginia and her mother arrived at the hospital. A lady in a pink uniform was waiting with a wheelchair. She asked Virginia to ride in the wheelchair to her room. "This is fun!" thought Virginia as the lady pushed her wheelchair onto the elevator.

A smiling nurse greeted Virginia when she arrived at her hospital room. The nurse was so kind and cheerful that Virginia soon began to feel that she had known the nurse for a long time. In just a few minutes the nurse and her mother had helped Virginia put on a hospital gown.

Another nurse came into the room carrying a funny-looking tray with lots of glass tubes and bottles on it. "I need to take your blood sample," said the new nurse. She asked Virginia to hold out her hand.

"Yeoow!" yelled Virginia, as the nurse quickly stuck the end of Virginia's finger with a needle. A small bright red drop appeared on her finger.

"I'm sorry to hurt you," said the nurse.

Virginia was beginning to think this wasn't so much fun after all. She decided it really wasn't fun when another nurse gave her a shot which was supposed to make her sleepy. Virginia lay back on her bed and began to fuss about people "hurting" her, but she went to sleep right in the middle of a sentence.

Just then two men in green clothes came with a long padded cart on wheels. They gently placed the sleeping girl on the cart and took her to the operating room.

When Virginia woke up, she was back in her bed. Her stomach was sore, and she seemed to have a difficult time waking up. "The operation is over," said her mother, leaning over the bed.

But Virginia just said "Oh," and went back to sleep.

Later when Virginia awoke again, there was a man in the room talking to her parents. "Hello, Virginia," he said, "I'm Chaplain Morris, the hospital chaplain. That means I'm a minister, and I spend all my time with families and patients here at the hospital." Chaplain Morris talked with Virginia for a few minutes, and then he asked her parents to stand with him beside Virginia's bed. Chaplain Morris held Virginia's hand while he prayed.

During the next few days, several people, including her pastor and Sunday School teacher, came to visit Virginia. Some people brought gifts, and some just came to see how she was feeling. By the time Virginia left the hospital, she had decided that the hospital wasn't so bad after all.

Story Questions: Why did the school nurse call Mrs. Sowell? What did the doctor say was wrong with Virginia? How did Virginia feel when told she would have to have an operation? How did Virginia get to her hospital room? What made Virginia yell? Who was in the room when she woke up? What did the chaplain do? Who visited Virginia?

Scripture Passage: "I was sick, and ye visited me" (Matt. 25:36).

Scripture Question: Why is it helpful to visit people when they are sick?

Scripture Comment for Parents: The Scripture sentence quoted above comes from a portion of the Bible where Jesus tells about the day of judgment. Jesus said some people will be blessed because they visited the Lord at a time of "sickness." He said the people would be surprised because they would not have realized they had visited the Lord at such a time. The response to the people would be, "Inasmuch as ye have done it unto one of the least of these my brethren, ye have done it unto me" (Matt. 25:40). Visiting the sick out of genuine concern and love is like doing the same for Jesus.

Prayer Suggestion: Pray for someone you know who is in the hospital.

Follow-up Activity: Play hospital. You can make IV bottles with soft drink bottles, string, and masking tape. Oxygen masks may be fashioned of a jump rope and a wire strainer. Boxes and tape make believable casts. Pretend experiences such as this help make real experiences less frightening later on.

WILLIAM'S BROTHER

Food Suggestion: Mother's choice.

Action Activity: Lay newspapers on the floor. Have each child lay down on the newspapers. Draw an outline of their bodies. Children may wish to color the outlines.

Song Time: Include "Jesus Loves the Little Children."

Interest Item: Picture of a group of children.

Listening Preparation Question: What kind of school did Donnie attend?

Story: "Why does your brother walk funny?" asked Ashley. "He looks older than us, but he walks like a two-year-old, and he talks funny too."

William answered, "Donnie is retarded. When he was born

somehow he didn't get enough oxygen in his brain, and part of it was hurt real bad. My dad says it's a miracle that he can walk at all."

"Does he go to school?" asked Ashley.

"He goes to a special school for kids with learning problems," said William.

"If he goes to school for a long time and works real hard, will he be like us then?" asked Ashley.

"No," William shook his head. "The special education teacher thinks that someday Donnie will be able to take care of himself—like getting dressed and feeding himself. But probably he never will read or do math very well."

"Are all retarded kids like Donnie?" asked Ashley.

"Not at all," replied William. "There are many kinds of retardation problems, and each child is different. Some can do lots of things, and others not so much."

"Does it bother you that your brother is retarded?" inquired Ashley.

"Well, I wish he wasn't," replied William. "Mom and Dad have to spend extra time with him, and that's hard on all of us. I guess the worst thing is that sometimes kids laugh at Donnie. You know, Ashley, just because he is retarded, it doesn't mean that Donnie's feelings are retarded. Yesterday he came into the house crying because the Blake girls were making fun of him. I wanted to go out and beat them up, but Mom wouldn't let me. She said it wouldn't do any good."

Both children sat quietly for a moment, and then William said, "But Donnie is lots of fun, too. And he loves all of his family. My grandmother says that Donnie is so special because he loves us so much and doesn't expect anything in return."

"What can I do for Donnie?" asked Ashley.

"For one thing, be nice to him. If he acts like a little kid, remember that's just the way he is. And don't make a big deal out of it."

"I wonder why God made retarded people," said Ashley.

"I asked our pastor that once," said William.

"What did he say?" asked Ashley.

"He said that he didn't know why, but he knew that just as Jesus loved the little children, he had a special place in his heart for retarded people."

"I'm going to talk to the Blake girls. I'm sure that they just don't understand about retarded people," said Ashley. "I guess they just didn't realize that Donnie has feelings too."

"Thanks," said William. "Come on, let's help Donnie into the house."

Story Questions: What was wrong with Donnie? Would Donnie ever be like the other kids? Are all retarded children like Donnie? What made Donnie cry? Does he ever have fun? What can you do for retarded people?

Scripture Passage: "But Jesus said, Suffer little children, and forbid them not, to come unto me: for of such is the kingdom of heaven" (Matt. 19:14).

Scripture Question: Did Jesus like little children?

Scripture Comment for Parents: The King James Version of this verse does *not* mean that Jesus intended for children to suffer. The word *suffer* in King James's day meant "to permit." Actually Jesus was saying, "Permit little children, and forbid them not, to come unto me." All children, including retarded children, are precious to Jesus. Retarded children have the qualities of trust, faith, and innocence of which Jesus must have been speaking when he said, "of such is the kingdom of heaven."

Prayer Suggestion: Pray for the family of a retarded child in your community.

Follow-up Activity: Visit a Sunday School class for retarded children. If you have friends with a retarded child, invite them to visit your home and bring the child. Many such families are shunned. They would welcome an invitation which includes their *entire* family.

SHARING COOKIES

Food Suggestion: Cookies and milk.

Action Activity: Draw yourself. Hold a piece of paper over each child's face. Give him a crayon and have him draw his own face on the paper. Compare pictures. See if you can guess who's who.

Song Time: Include "Praise Him! Praise Him!"

Interest Item: Box of cookies.

Listening Preparation Question: What person said, "I do love to share."

Story: Holly skipped up the steps of the nursing home with the rest of her Sunday School class.

"I wonder what it's going to be like?" she whispered to Josh. "I've never been in a nursing home before."

"Neither have I," replied Josh.

Inside the door the class waited while Mrs. Sharp talked to the lady who was going to show them around.

"Now class," said Mrs. Sharp, "we are going to see Mrs. Steadman. She is a member of our church and years ago she taught me in Sunday School."

"She must really be old," whispered Josh.

The children started walking down the hall. Each room had two beds with a hospital curtain between them. Some of the rooms had flowers in the windows and almost all had television sets.

"Be careful, children, and walk on the side of the hall," said Mrs. Sharp as they passed a man who had a metal walker in front of him.

"What's that?" asked Josh.

"I broke my hip last winter," replied the man smiling. "This walker helps me so that I won't fall again." The man patted Josh on the head and went on down the hall.

"This is Mrs. Steadman's room," said Mrs. Sharp. "Let's go in, sing, and give her the cookies we made."

Mrs. Steadman was sitting in a wheelchair. Holly was a little bit afraid. She didn't know any older people and she didn't know what to say.

"Hello, children," said Mrs. Steadman. "I am so glad you came to see me."

"We would like to sing for you," said Mrs. Sharp. Holly and the other children started to sing. Mrs. Steadman smiled and nodded her head to the music.

Holly watched her face. "Why, she is a nice lady," she whispered to Josh.

"Holly, would you give Mrs. Steadman the cookies?" asked Mrs. Sharp.

"Oh, thank you, children. There are so many, won't you help me eat them?"

The children shook their heads and said, "No, they are for you!" Mrs. Steadman looked sad, thought Holly.

Holly said quickly, "I'd like one."

"Good!" said Mrs. Steadman as she held out the box. "You know I can't get out and buy things for people and I do love to share."

Now the other boys and girls each took a cookie from the box. There were several left after they had all taken one. "I'll share these with the nurses tonight," she said.

"Let's sing one more song before we go," said Mrs. Sharp. "How about 'Praise Him! Praise Him!'?" The children sang out. Other patients came into the hall to hear them.

"Come again to see us," said Mrs. Steadman as the children started to leave.

"We will!" they all said.

"You know," said Holly, "we came to cheer her up and give her cookies and she made us happy too."

"I have a good feeling inside," said Josh. "Let's ask Mrs. Sharp if we can come back soon."

Story Questions: Where did the Sunday School class go? What were some of the things they saw at the nursing home?

What did the class do at the nursing home? What did Mrs. Steadman want to do for the class? How did Holly feel as they left Mrs. Steadman?

Scripture Passage: "Jesus . . . went about doing good" (Acts 10:38).

Scripture Question: What were some of the good things done by Jesus?

Scripture Comment for Parents: Jesus often used sad or unpleasant situations to show that goodness could be found in even the worst of conditions. In so doing he set an example for all of his followers. We are not to accept any bad situation at face value, but we are to seek opportunities for doing good— opportunities which may not be obvious, but, nonetheless, are there. A nursing home is not always a cheerful place, but it does provide many opportunities for sharing and receiving love.

Prayer Suggestion: Pray for someone you know who is in a nursing home. Ask God to help you find ways to share love with that person.

Follow-up Activity: Make cookies or take fruit to a nursing home patient. Your church should be able to give you the name of someone to visit if you do not know anyone personally.

Personal Worth

A WHOLE YEAR OLDER

Food Suggestion: Children's choice.

Action Activity: Let each child take turns shaving. Give each child enough shaving cream to cover his face and let him use a spoon as a razor. (Child holds bowl of spoon in his hand and shaves with the handle.) Little girls will enjoy this activity as much as boys.

Song Time: Include "Footsteps of Jesus."

Interest Item: A bathing suit.

Listening Preparation Question: What group had John been with last year?

Story: "Are you going to take swimming lessons this week, John?" asked Alan, the lifeguard.

"You bet," replied John, "this year I'm going to go off the diving board!"

"That will be a real achievement over last year, won't it?" laughed Alan.

All the boys and girls were lined up on the side of the pool.

"Beep," went Alan's whistle. "Now, all of you who have had swimming lessons before come with me," said Alan. "The rest of you stay with Mary Jo down here at the two-foot end."

John and several others followed Alan to the five-foot section of the pool.

"Hold on to the side but jump in and get wet," said Alan. John was a little scared, but not as scared as last year. "Now," said Alan, "let's bob and blow bubbles."

"Here it comes," thought John. He held his breath and under the water he went. "Why, I'm not scared at all!"

"John," laughed Alan, "you look surprised. Did you think you were going to be scared like you were last year? Remember, you are a whole year older." Alan blew his whistle again. "Everyone out of the pool," he said.

As they sat on the side of the pool John watched the little kids down in the shallow end. Last year he had been one of them.

At the end of the two-week session, Alan said to the group, "I expect you to be able to swim across the pool and back, and to be able to go off the low diving board."

Some of the kids groaned. John thought to himself, "I think I can do it. Dad said if you make up your mind to do something you can do it. I'm going to!"

Every day John was able to swim a little better. He had trouble making his arms and legs work at the same time while keeping his head down, but he practiced hard.

Finally Alan said, "Today we are going to the ten-foot section and swim across. After that we will take turns on the diving board."

John waited. "I know I can, I know I can," he said over and over again. He felt the hot sun on his back but somehow he felt cold inside.

"Okay, John, across the pool," said Alan. John jumped in. "Why, it's just like the shallow end as long as you don't think about your feet being so far from the bottom," thought John, as he climbed out the other side.

"Now to the board," said Alan, "remember, knees bent, arms out, and head down."

John stood, his head down, and his arms outstretched, "I'm scared," he thought, "but here goes." Splash!

"You'll never win a gold medal with that dive," laughed Alan, "but you sure have come a long way since last summer."

John felt so good inside. "Next year I'll go off the high dive," he said.

Story Questions: What was John determined to do this year for the first time? How was John surprised when he put his head under the water? What advice had John's father given him? Did John go off the diving board? What was he determined to do next year?

Scripture Passage: "And Jesus increased in wisdom and stature, and in favour with God and man" (Luke 2:52).

Scripture Question: This verse tells of the ways that Jesus grew when he was young. What do you think it means to grow in "wisdom and stature"?

Scripture Comment for Parents: It is important for adults and children alike to remember that children are constantly developing. What they could not do last year, they either can do now or else will be able to do in the future. Even Jesus went through the same developmental stages as other children. He grew physically (stature) and intellectually (wisdom). Also he "increased in favour with God and man." Parents not only have the opportunity to help a child grow physically through good exercise, but also to grow in knowledge, in spiritual relationship with God, and in personal relationships with others. These avenues of growth can be observed and measured as readily as can physical growth.

Prayer Suggestion: Ask God to help you set goals for growth in your relationship with him.

Follow-up Activity: Have each child demonstrate some skill they have mastered in the past year. It may be tying shoelaces, learning to read, or play an instrument. Many times children feel there are so many things they can't do that both parent and child overlook what has been mastered.

SEEING GOD'S WORLD

Food Suggestion: Maple syrup and ice cream.

Action Activity: Play "Riddle, Riddle, Marie, I See Something You Don't See, and the Color of It Is _____."

Song Time: Include "This Is My Father's World."

Interest Item: "Little House" books.

Listening Preparation Question: What did Laura do after school each day?

Story: Laura Ingalls Wilder, author of the "Little House" books, is beloved by children and adults around the world.

Mrs. Wilder's descriptions are so real you feel that you are there with her. While reading about the making of maple syrup in the Wisconsin woods, you can smell the maple syrup and taste its sweet stickiness on your tongue. When Laura tells of blizzards in the Dakota territory, you can hear the wolves howl and almost feel the cold wind at your back. Your face tingles as the blowing snow starts coming down faster and faster.

Laura Ingalls Wilder had a great deal of practice in describing things. After her sister Mary went blind, Laura became her eyes. The girls would take long walks on the prairie. Laura would describe the clouds and the wild flowers. She would try to help Mary see the wind rippling through the prairie grass. In the afternoon after school, Laura would relive the day's events for Mary, who had to stay at home. All this practice in describing things later made Laura Ingalls Wilder a great writer.

So often we do not really see the things around us. Most of us have two good eyes to see God's beautiful world, and yet we often don't really look at its loveliness.

Story Questions: Who is the story about? What was special about the descriptions she wrote in her books? How did she learn to describe things so well? How should we use our eyes?

Scripture Passage: "The heavens declare the glory of God; and the firmament sheweth his handiwork" (Ps. 19:1).

Scripture Question: Give some examples of God's handiwork in nature.

Scripture Comment for Parents: The beauty of the heavens (sky) with its sun, moon, stars, and clouds serve as a continual reminder of the greatness of God. The word *firmament* also referred to the sky. (See Gen. 1:14-17.) This verse reminds us that God created all the beauty we see above our heads outdoors. God's handiwork is all that he has made.

Prayer Suggestion: Thank God for the ability to see his beautiful world and for the beauty around us.

Follow-up Activity: Blindfold one family member and then have another family member describe things around the room or out the window. Take turns being blindfolded. Other family members may each act out an event and let someone describe it to the blindfolded person.

THE SENSES GAME

Food Suggestion: Popcorn. Let the child help make it.

Action Activity: Place a number of different objects in a box. Cover the box with a cloth. Family members take turns guessing what is in the box by putting one hand under the cloth and feeling an object.

Song Time: Sing action songs which involve such movement as clapping hands, standing up and sitting down, and marching.

Interest Item: Use the box of objects as the interest item.

Listening Preparation Question: This story will be about five things God has given to us. Which ones did you use to enjoy the popcorn?

Story: One summer afternoon Mark and Lucy were sitting in the front yard. "I wish we had something different to do," said Lucy. "We do the same old thing every day."

"Let's play the senses game," said Mark.

"What's that?" asked Lucy.

"We learned it at Sunday School," said Mark. "God has given us five senses: touch, taste, see, hear, and smell. We'll take turns telling each of them."

"Oh," said Lucy, "I smell the rose bushes and taste the bubble gum."

"And I see a bug on your arm and I hear you yelling," laughed Mark, rolling on the grass.

"Smarty," said Lucy, "I am touching this grass and I am going to throw some of it on you."

"Don't," yelled Mark, "then I will feel mother brushing it out of my hair."

"You know, Mark, I can hear the tinkle of a little bell," said Lucy, "and I think I can see the ice cream truck."

"Boy," said Mark, "I can't wait to taste a Popsicle."

After Lucy went to bed that night, she started thinking again about the senses game. "Wouldn't it be terrible," she said to herself, "not to be able to see, or hear, or taste, or smell." Then snuggling under the soft covers, she said, "Oh yes, and feel."

Story Questions: What are the five things God has given? What was the "senses game"? What were some of the ways that the boy and girl in the story used their senses? Do you know anyone who does not have any one of the senses? What problems do they have because of lacking one of the senses? How could we help someone in that condition?

Scripture Passage: "The hearing ear, and the seeing eye, the Lord hath made even both of them" (Prov. 20:12).

Scripture Questions: What senses are mentioned in this verse? Who gave us those senses?

Scripture Comment for Parents: This verse reminds us that God has given us the ability to see and to hear. We are to give thanks to God for all of our senses, and we should use them only in ways that please him.

Prayer Suggestion: Give thanks to God for your ability to see, hear, touch, smell, and taste.

Follow-up Activity: Play the senses game.

HANDS

Food Suggestion: Finger foods, such as cheese cubes, crackers, and carrot sticks.

Action Activities: Bob for apples.

Song Time: Include a song of thanksgiving such as "Count Your Blessings."

Interest Item: Draw an outline of a hand.

Listening Preparation Question: How did Joyce's brother want her to eat dinner?

Story: "Wash your hands before supper," called Mother from the kitchen.

"Sometimes I wish I didn't have any hands. I get tired of washing them all the time," grumbled Joyce.

"Sure would be hard to eat without them," said Joel, Joyce's big brother. "Hey, Mom, let's let Joyce try to eat without her hands tonight. She says she doesn't want them any more."

"Stop it, Joel, I'm hungry," cried Joyce. "I'll wash my hands."

After the blessing Joyce's father said, "You know, I guess we aren't thankful enough that God gave us hands. I sure would hate to do without them."

"Yes," said Joel, "paws are OK for animals but fingers sure work better for picking up things."

"Like food, Joel? Please use your fork and not your fingers to eat your meat!" said Mother.

Joyce laughed. "Remember the time on Halloween when we bobbed for apples and I got a nose full of water and got my hair all wet?"

"Can you think of any other reasons you are glad to have hands?" asked Father.

"Well, we can feel and touch things," said Joyce. "I like to feel things that are soft or smooth."

"Blind people read with their fingers from Braille books," said Joel.

"True," said Mother, "and some deaf people use hand sign language to talk to each other. Why, I'm using my hands to talk to you right now. Have you ever tried to talk to someone while sitting on your hands? It is hard to do."

"God expects us to use our hands," said Father. "He expects us to work with them and to help others as well. No other creature on earth has hands as wonderfully made as ours. He gave them to us for a purpose."

"But Daddy," said Joyce, "my hands are so small!"

"I know," said Father, "they may not be as big or as strong as grown-up hands, but they still are perfectly made in every way. You know how to do many things with them already. You can write and draw and dress yourself. There are many things you can do for others already."

"You're right, Daddy" said Joyce. "I wouldn't like it if I didn't have hands."

Story Questions: Why did Joyce wish she had no hands? What are some of the ways we use our hands? How does God expect us to use our hands?

Scripture Passage: "Lift up your hands in the sanctuary, and bless the Lord" (Psalm 134:2).

Scripture Question: What is the sanctuary?

Scripture Comment for Parents: This verse depicts still another way we can use our hands—lift them in praise of God. The leaders of worship in ancient Israel would raise their hands in the sanctuary, the holy place, on behalf of all the people. Perhaps the raising of the hands was a symbolic way of receiving God's blessings.

Prayer Suggestion: Thank God for your hands. Ask God to help you use your hands in ways that please him.

Follow-up Activity: Carry on a conversation while sitting on your hands, or obtain sign language instructions and practice talking in sign language.

BETTER THAN OTHERS

Food Suggestion: Ice cream sundaes.

Action Activity: If the weather and the time of day is right, go outside and play catch. If not, play in the house with a small foam rubber ball.

Song Time: Include "Have Faith in God."

Interest Item: A ball.

Listening Preparation Question: Did anyone make fun of Shirley?

Story: "Daddy, I don't think I want to play on a softball team anymore," said Shirley.

"Now, Shirley, you know that we told you when you started playing ball you would have to play the whole season. If you don't want to play next year, that's another story."

"But I'm not very good and I make outs and I can't catch the ball," said Shirley, with tears in her eyes.

"Did anyone say anything to you because you missed that ball in the third inning?" asked Dad.

"No, but I can't play as well as Nina and Ruth, and I want to quit."

"Shirley, quitting because someone is a better player than you won't solve anything."

"But Daddy, I'll never be as good as they are if I practiced a thousand years!" said Shirley.

"Maybe not, both Nina and Ruth are really good players. But it takes more than two players to make a team. Remember that in the fifth inning when you made it to second base you knocked in a run," answered Daddy.

Shirley grinned, "I guess I did. I forgot that. Daddy, how come God lets some people do things better than other people? It doesn't seem fair!"

"Whew! You know how to ask hard questions, that's for sure," said Daddy. "God gives us all certain abilities and some people try harder and therefore do better. And, Shirley, some people just seem to always do better."

"I remember when I was about your age, there was a boy who lived across the street. We were the same age but he was bigger, stronger, and smarter. He even acted better. It seemed to me that he was perfect. I was so jealous of him. One day I asked my dad, your grandfather, the same question, Shirley, and you know what he told me?"

"What," asked Shirley, wide-eyed because it had never occurred to her that anyone could do anything better than her father.

"Your granddaddy told me that he knew the other boy was good in most everything but that didn't matter. He told me that he loved me because I was me, his son. He also said that God loved me not because I was perfect in any way but just because I was me, his son also."

"You love me too, don't you, Daddy," said Shirley.

"You know I do, Shirley, and so does God love you just because you are you."

"Daddy, can we go outside and practice catching a few balls?" asked Shirley.

Story Questions: What did Shirley want to do? Why? What did her Dad remind her about playing the full season? What did he tell her when she complained about not being as good as the others? What does God think of us if others can do things better than we can?

Scripture Passage: "So we, being many, are one body in Christ . . . Having then gifts differing according to the grace that is given to us" (Rom. 12:5-6).

Scripture Question: What do you think the word *gifts* means?

Scripture Comment for Parents: Children may understand this verse better if they realize that the word *gifts* refers to a person's talents or abilities. All Christians have the same

Lord, but they have different abilities with which to serve the Lord. And not all Christians with the same talents have an equal degree of ability. We should not dwell on how much better or worse we do something in comparison with someone else. Instead, we ought to focus on our common faith in Christ, and then do the best we can.

Prayer Suggestion: Pray that God will help you to develop your own unique abilities to their fullest potential.

Follow-up Activity: Talk with children about a skill they would like to improve. Concentrate for one week on that skill. Help the child whenever possible. At the end of the week measure his improvement. Impress on him the idea that the best measurement is against yourself, not someone else.

Family Experiences

THE LOOSE TOOTH

Food Suggestion: Corn on the cob or apples.

Action Activity: Play follow-the-leader, with each member of the family taking turns as leader.

Song Time: No matter what time of the year, include "All I Want for Christmas Is My Two Front Teeth."

Interest Item: Baby teeth, if you have kept them.

Listening Preparation Question: What was Kim afraid would happen to her?

Story: Mom's supper smelled so good, and Kim was hungry. "I fixed corn on the cob just for you, Kim," said Mother. "Call Daddy and Stephen to the table."

After Daddy had said the blessing, Mother passed Kim the corn. "Watch it! It's hot," she said. Kim filled her plate with other food, but mostly she wanted to eat the corn.

"Eeoow!" yelled Kim as she bit into her corn. "My tooth."

"Looks like our baby is growing up," smiled Dad. "Got a loose tooth, Kim?"

As the days went by, Kim's tooth got looser and looser. "Let me see your tooth," said Mother.

"Don't pull it!" cried Kim.

"Why not?" asked Mother.

Kim started crying. "I don't want to be like Grandmother and have false teeth," she sobbed.

"Why Kim," said Mother, "you won't have to have false teeth. Remember that Stephen's teeth came out and new ones came back in."

"But why didn't Grandmother's teeth come back?" asked Kim.

"God has made us so that we have two sets of teeth," replied Mother, "a small set for when we are small, and a bigger set for when we are older. Hopefully, if we brush our teeth and visit the dentist, we won't ever have to have false teeth."

"You mean I am going to get a new tooth in place of the old wiggly one?" asked Kim.

"Yes, dear. After that tooth is out, in a few weeks, a new, bigger tooth will start to come in."

"Will I lose all my teeth I have now?"

"Yes, but not all at once," explained Kim's mother. "God made our bodies so that over a period of years we lose our baby teeth and then grown-up teeth come in."

"God is great," said Kim.

"He surely is," said Mother, "but he expects us to help take care of our bodies, too. We must watch what we eat, brush our teeth, and see our dentist as well. Part of showing God that we love him is in taking care of our bodies which he has so wonderfully made."

"I guess losing teeth isn't so bad after all," smiled Kim, "but I still wish that I could eat corn on the cob."

"I know," said Mother, "but you can next summer. And for right now we'll just cut the corn off the cob."

"Like my teeth," giggled Kim.

"Yes," laughed Mother, "like your teeth."

Story Questions: Why did Kim not want to be like her grandmother? What did Kim learn about how God made us?

What would help us keep the adult teeth God gives us? How is taking care of our bodies one way we can show God we love him?

Scripture Passage: "I will praise thee; for I am fearfully and wonderfully made: marvellous are thy works; and that my soul knoweth right well" (Ps. 139:14).

Scripture Question: Why should a person praise God?

Scripture Comment for Parents: The writer of this verse apparently became very sensitive to the greatness and uniqueness of his own body. He realized that the ability to walk, talk, and grasp were special abilities given to each person. He may not have been aware of all the special features about the body, such as the ability to maintain the same temperature despite extreme heat or cold, but he would have known enough about the body to realize what a tremendous work God did in creating people. Like a person expressing delight in seeing a beautiful flower or a spectacular sunset, the writer was so overwhelmed by what God had done that he could not help but praise God.

Prayer Suggestion: Give thanks to God for creating you with so many beautiful and wonderful characteristics. Ask him to help you take proper care of your body.

Follow-up Activity: Look at a tooth chart in the encyclopedia or baby book. Talk with children about their first baby tooth. Possibly show them teeth prints they have left on furniture.

THE BOY WHO NEVER GOT TO DO ANYTHING

Food Suggestion: Youngest child's choice. If the youngest child is too young to talk, then choose his favorite food. Even baby food fruit in jars and graham crackers are fun.

Action Activity: Have a balloon burst. See who can blow up a balloon, sit on it, and pop it. Younger children may have to have help blowing up balloon but should have no trouble popping it!

Song Time: Each family member take turns choosing a song.

Interest Item: Pictures of your family.

Listening Preparation Question: Why was Bruce unhappy?

Story: Tears streamed down Bruce's face as he watched his two sisters get out of the car. Both girls had packs on their backs and were carrying sleeping bags. They were greeted by a gang of other noisy, giggling girls who had arrived at the Girl Scout camp before them. Some of the girls apparently remembered his older sister from camp last year. They all were talking about how much fun they were going to have for the next two weeks.

The two sisters turned and waved at Bruce and their parents, and then hurried into the camp office.

On the way back home, the car seemed very lonesome and quiet. Finally, Bruce could hold back no longer. He suddenly started crying out loud.

"Why what in the world is wrong, Bruce?" asked his mother as she turned around in the front seat. At first Bruce couldn't say anything. He just sobbed uncontrollably. His mother told him to climb over into the front seat and sit in her lap. "Now tell me what's wrong," she said again. Still Bruce couldn't say anything. "Is it because your sisters are gone?" his mother inquired.

Bruce shook his head no and then blurted out, "I never get to do anything!"

"What do you mean?" asked his father.

"The girls get to go camping and do lots of other things I don't get to do."

"That's true," said his mother, "But when they were your age they didn't get to do the things they are doing now either. When you get to be as old as they are, you'll get to do more things too."

"One thing I'm going to do for sure is go to Girl Scout camp— I mean Boy Scout camp," he quickly corrected himself. His mother and father laughed, and Bruce was so embarrassed that he felt like crying again.

"All right," his mother said quickly, "you can go to camp when you are older. But let's think about the things you get to do now."

"I don't get to do anything." pouted Bruce.

"I'm not so sure about that," replied Father. "What about your baseball team?"

"That's just one thing," said Bruce.

"Yes," said Mother, "and another 'one thing' is your Sunday School class at church. And don't forget the picnic your class is having tomorrow afternoon."

"I guess I would have to remember getting to ride my bike, and playing with Jeff and Craig," said Bruce, reluctantly. "But I still don't think it's fair that the girls get to do something special and I don't!"

"Oh, but you will get to do something special. In fact, almost everything you do while they are gone will be special," said Mother.

"What do you mean?" asked Bruce, with a puzzled look on his face.

"During the two weeks the girls are in camp your father and I will have you all to ourselves. You won't have to fuss with anyone about who your father will play with first when he comes home from work. You won't even have to take turns choosing which television program to watch."

That night when Bruce said his prayers, he asked God to be with his sisters at camp, and then he said, "Thank you, God, for special times when we can have home all to ourselves."

Story Questions: What were Bruce's sisters going to do? What did Bruce do after leaving his sisters at camp? Why did he think he never got to do anything? What were some of the things he did get to do? What was special about the two weeks his sisters were at camp?

Scripture Passage: "And he said unto him, Son, thou art ever with me, and all that I have is thine" (Luke 15:31).

Scripture Question: These words were spoken by a father to his son. What was special about what the father told the son?

Scripture Comment for Parents: This verse comes at the conclusion of the parable of the prodigal son. The verse should remind us, as God's children, that our heavenly Father is with us always, and that all of his great power and love is ours also for the asking.

Prayer Suggestion: Pray that God will make you more aware of his blessings in your life.

Follow-up Activity: Sometime this week try to give your child an hour of your undivided attention. If you have more than one child consider letting each child have a turn staying up one hour after regular bedtime to have their own special time alone with their parents.

THE OLDEN DAYS

Food Suggestion: Banana pudding.
Action Activity: Play charades, using titles of songs.
Song Time: Include songs parents sung as children.
Interest Item: Light bulb.
Listening Preparation Question: What did they do without television in the "olden days"?

Story: "I think we are going to have quite a storm," said Dad, as he came in the kitchen. Just then the rain started to come down. Jeremy could hear it on the window.

"I guess I had better put our bikes in the garage," he said, running to the door.

"Make sure you pick up your ball glove too," said Mother.

"Better tell Betsy to come home from Elaine's," said Dad.

Just then Betsy ran into the yard. "Here, put your bike up," said Jeremy.

Both children ran inside just as the rain started pouring down. "Whew, that was a close call," said Jeremy. All of a sudden there was a bright flash of light and then BOOM! The lights flickered. BOOM again. The lights went out.

"That sounds like lightning hit the transformer," said Dad. "We may not have electricity for several hours."

"I'm glad I had supper ready," said Mother. "I'm not sure raw hamburger would taste very good."

"Let's have candles," said Betsy.

"Fine," said Mother. "They are on the second shelf in the cabinet by the door."

"If the electricity stays off long," said Jeremy, "I won't be able to see television before I go to bed. What am I going to do?"

"I think it is a little too dark to read and we aren't used to reading by candlelight," said Dad. I guess we could play games.

"Just like they did in the 'olden days'?" asked Betsy.

"When?" asked Mother.

"You know how they used to do. Grandmother told me that when she was a little girl, before television, that her family used to play games together and then read the Bible and pray together."

Mother and Dad looked at each other. "I guess we could pretend we live in the 'olden days,'" said Mother, smiling.

"I want to play charades," said Jeremy. "Let's act out song titles. I'm first!" Jeremy held up three fingers.

"Three words," said Betsy.

Jeremy nodded and held up three fingers again.

"Three something," said Dad.

Jeremy jumped up and down. He put his hands over his eyes.

"I know! I know!" said Betsy, " 'Three Blind Mice!' Now it's my turn." The family played several more rounds.

Dad said, "It's getting late. Betsy, you said Grandmother said they read the Bible and prayed together?"

"Yes, that's what she told me," replied Betsy.

"OK, I think I can see well enough to read by this candle," said Dad. Betsy and Jeremy sat very still as Dad read the Bible. "Now let's each pray. Jeremy, you start and I will close," said

Dad. "And Betsy, I want to thank you for a wonderful idea. It has been really great having an 'olden days' time together."

Story Questions: Why did the lights go out? What did they use for lights? What was the name of the game they played? Who prayed following the reading of the Bible? Would what they did in the "olden days" be good to do today?

Scripture Passage: "They received the word with all readiness of mind, and searched the scriptures daily" (Acts 17:11).

Scripture Question: What did the people do each day?

Scripture Comment for Parents: Paul and Silas were traveling from place to place preaching about Christ. At Thessalonica, certain people refused to consider that what was preached might be true. These people caused a disturbance which forced the two missionaries to leave. The Bible says that the people in the next town of Berea "were more noble than those in Thessalonica." The Bereans listened to the missionaries, and they studied the Scriptures to be certain the missionaries were speaking the truth. As a result of "searching the scriptures" and listening to the two men, many were saved.

Prayer Suggestion: Give thanks to God for his written revelation, and ask for his leadership in daily Bible readings.

Follow-up Activity: Have your own "olden days" time together. Spend an entire evening without television, and if you are really brave, turn off the lights.

The Piano Lesson

Food Suggestion: Try a food new to the market. Explain to the children that many snack-type items were not available when you were a child.

Action Activity: Fill several bottles or glasses the same size with graduated amounts of water. Each bottle or glass when tapped will have a different pitch. Try to play a tune on the bottles. Take turns.

Song Time: Include a hymn you sang at church last Sunday.

Interest Item: The musical bottles.

Listening Preparation Question: What did Stacy expect to do after her first piano lesson?

Story: Stacy liked to sit close to the front of the sanctuary during the worship service. From there she could see the choir and her pastor. But best of all she could watch Mrs. Wright play the piano.

Stacy watched with envy as Mrs. Wright's fingers seemed to know just where to go. She didn't ever seem to make a mistake.

This Sunday she watched with particular interest. "I'm going to take piano lessons from Mrs. Wright, Tuesday," Stacy whispered to Brenda.

Brenda's eyes widened. "I wish I could take piano lessons, too!" she said.

"Then ask your Mother to talk to Mrs. Wright," Stacy whispered.

Tuesday afternoon finally came. Now Stacy was scared! She looked at her fingers. She hoped that they could somehow play the piano.

"OK, let's get started, Stacy," said Mrs. Wright. "First let me give you your piano books." Mrs. Wright placed a book in front of Stacy. It had notes on it like she had learned in her choir group at church.

"Now," said Mrs. Wright, "let me show you where to place your fingers."

Soon the lesson was over. "Now Stacy, I want you to practice every day. That is the most difficult thing about piano lessons. Everyone wants to be able to play, but only those who are willing to practice ever really learn to play well."

Stacy nodded.

When she got home Stacy showed her mother her new piano books. "Stacy, you look disappointed," said Mother. "I thought you wanted to take piano lessons."

"I do, Mother," said Stacy, "But these songs don't sound

like the songs Mrs. Wright plays." A tear started to slowly run down Stacy's cheek.

"Why Stacy," said Mother putting her arm around her. "You can't expect to learn in one lesson or even in one year how to play as well as Mrs. Wright. It takes time and practice to learn to play the piano."

"Mrs. Wright said I should practice every day," said Stacy, sniffing.

"You know, I think God has given you a talent to play the piano," said Mother. "You have been able to pick out tunes on the xylophone for some time. But even as God gives us talents he expects us to put forth some work to develop them."

"I wish I could play the piano right now!" said Stacy.

"Then go do it," said Mother. "Don't expect to sound like Mrs. Wright. But you can know that each time you practice you will be better than the last time. Now, let's hear what you have learned."

Story Questions: What did Stacy like to watch at church? What did she do at her first piano lesson? What did Mrs. Wright tell Stacy she would have to do to learn to play the piano? Why was Stacy disappointed? What does God expect us to do with our talents?

Scripture Passage: "And so he that had received five talents came and brought other five talents, saying, Lord, thou deliveredst unto me five talents: behold, I have gained beside them five talents more" (Matt. 25:20). (Note: The word *talent* in this verse refers to a type of money used in New Testament times.)

Scripture Question: What does God expect us to do with the abilities he has given to us?

Scripture Comment for Parents: Though the parable of the talents deals with investing money, it illustrates what God expects of us in terms of investing our abilities. God gives us various abilities, and he expects us to work to develop them to the fullest potential. He expects us to invest those abilities in service for him.

Prayer Suggestion: Give thanks for your various God-given abilities, and pray that you would have the determination to fully develop those abilities.

Follow-up Activities: Take your child to talk with your church organist or pianist. Ask the musician how long she took lessons and how much she practiced as a child. How much does she practice now? If your child plays the piano, ask if he or she may play on the piano in your church. It might be best to find a time when no one else is in the building.

THE BIRTHDAY CELEBRATION

Food Suggestion: Cupcakes. Write each child's name in icing on a cupcake or use little candies to make their initials.

Action Activity: Play table tag. Blindfold two players. Stand them at opposite ends of a table. Both players must touch the table at all times. The person who is designated "it" must move around the table and try to tag the other player who is trying to stay out of his way. Take turns.

Song Time: Include "Joy to the World."

Interest Item: Package of birthday candles.

Listening Preparation Question: Why did Phyllis have an unhappy birthday?

Story: "Did we ever fool my sister, Phyllis, yesterday!" Rodney said to Elaine as they were walking home from school.

"What did you do?" asked Elaine, eagerly. She was always glad to hear how younger kids pulled tricks on older kids, and Phyllis was really older. She was in the sixth grade!

"Yesterday was Phyllis's birthday," said Rodney. "But when she got up in the morning, no one in the family said anything about it. We just acted like it was an ordinary day. At first she didn't say anything either. She sort of looked like she was expecting us to say 'surprise' any minute. Just before we left for school Phyllis did ask if anything unusual was planned for the day, but we all said 'of course not, why should there be?' Before she could say anything else I told her she'd better hurry up or we'd be late for school.

"By the end of supper last night she really thought we'd forgotten. She finally blurted out, 'Didn't anyone remember my birthday?' "

"What did you do then?" asked Elaine.

"Oh we had her fooled good by then," said Rodney. "We all said we were sorry to have forgotten, and that it was too late to go to the store to get any presents."

"Had you forgotten?" asked Elaine.

"Of course not, but we waited until she got into bed. She was sort of crying, but she cheered up quickly when we marched into her room with a cake and lots of presents. We really fooled her," laughed Rodney.

"I wouldn't want to have a birthday at your house," said Elaine.

"Why not?" said Rodney, "it was all in fun!"

"It sounds to me like everybody had fun except Phyllis. It must have been the most miserable day of her life," said Elaine.

"But it ended all right," retorted Rodney.

"Just the same," said Elaine, "I much prefer the way we celebrate birthdays at my house."

"Well Smarty," cracked Rodney, "what does your family do on birthdays?"

Elaine smiled as she remembered different birthday experiences. "At our house birthdays are fun for *everyone*. We call them days of celebration."

"What in the world is there to celebrate?" asked Rodney.

"We celebrate the fact that the person was born. We thank God for giving us that special person," explained Elaine.

"You're kidding," said Rodney.

"No, I'm not," said Elaine emphatically, "and we do it for the adults as well as the children."

"Just exactly what do you do," asked Rodney, who by now was very interested—especially since his birthday was next in his family.

"For one thing we talk about the birthday several days in advance. Oh, we tease the birthday person, but we tease them about guessing what we've already bought or made for them. Then on the day, we give them breakfast in bed, and we gather around their bed to watch them open the presents. Sometimes there is a party planned later for my sister or me, but we open family presents the first thing."

Rodney's eyes widened at the thought of starting the day with presents.

"All day long," Elaine continued, "we let the person know it is their special day. We try to do what they want to do. Mother fixes the birthday person's special food, even if the others don't like it. And then at bedtime we go back to the birthday person's room and each member of the family prays. We thank God for that person and for what the person means to us."

"Say," said Rodney, as he turned up the walk leading to his house, "I do like your birthday celebrations better than ours. I'm going to tell my folks about them now."

Story Questions: How did Phyllis's family treat her on her birthday? What did Phyllis think about the way her family fooled her? How did Elaine's family celebrate birthdays? Which way did Rodney like best? Which way do you like best? Why?

Scripture Passage: "For this child I prayed; and the Lord hath given me my petition which I asked of him" (1 Sam. 1:27).

Scripture Question: What had God given to the person who had prayed?

Scripture Comment for Parents: These words as recorded in 1 Samuel were spoken by Hannah, the mother of Samuel. For many years she had no children, and so she prayed earnestly for a child. Hannah had so strongly wanted a son that she vowed to God that her son would be dedicated to him. When God answered her prayer, Hannah kept her vow and dedicated Samuel to a lifetime of service to God. Hannah later gave birth to three more sons and two daughters. We do not know anything about these children, but we do know that each year Hannah made a new coat for Samuel—apparently a birthday present given as an expression of love.

Prayer Suggestion: Pray for each child in the family, asking that God would lead each child to become a dedicated follower of Christ.

Follow-up Activity: Through your school or church, find someone who has a birthday soon but who will not receive much recognition. This may be a child, older adult, or a shut-in. With your children plan a simple party for this person.

JACKIE'S WEDDING

Food Suggestion: Punch and cake. Make it a pretty, festive occasion.

Action Activity: Get ready for a wedding. Take turns fixing different hairstyles. If Mother doesn't mind, use some of her makeup. Boys may wish to try different ways to tie a necktie.

Song Time: Include songs that you know which might be sung at a wedding.

Interest Item: Parents' wedding pictures.

Listening Preparation Question: What did Jackie do at the wedding rehearsal?

Story: "I'm going to be in a wedding," Jackie announced to her friends at church.

"How can you be?" asked Marilyn, "you're not old enough to get married. You're not even old enough to go to school."

"I didn't say I was going to get married," replied Jackie. "I just said I was going to be in a wedding. My uncle is getting married, and I'm going to be the flower girl."

"What does a flower girl do?" asked Rachael.

"I'm not sure what all I'll do," answered Jackie, "but I do know I'll carry a basket of flowers. I'll find out more at the rehearsal tonight."

"What's a rehearsal?" asked Marilyn.

"I think it's when we practice the wedding," said Jackie.

That night Jackie went to the church where the wedding

was to take place. She was disappointed to learn that only
adults were at the church, and that there was no one for her
to play with. But she soon forgot her disappointment when
the pretty girl her uncle was marrying thanked her for being
the flower girl. She said that being a flower girl was very important, and that she knew Jackie would do a good job.

Jackie knew her job was important when she discovered that
she was to walk down the aisle just before the bride. She had
to practice walking several times, but she didn't mind because
everyone else had to practice their parts several times also.
Jackie did feel a little silly pretending to throw flowers, but
her uncle told her she would have lots of real flowers at the
wedding.

Practice for the wedding continued until everyone felt they
knew what they were to do. Then the minister asked them
all to be seated for a few minutes.

The minister said some funny things, which made everyone
laugh. Then he became very serious. He said that a wedding
was a happy occasion. The minister said that everyone who
had a part in the wedding ceremony was helping make the
ceremony a joyful experience because the couple only asked
those people who were special to them to be in the wedding.
He said the wedding also was a worship experience where
two people asked God to bless their marriage. Then he asked
everyone to bow their heads while he prayed. Jackie couldn't
remember all of the prayer, but it went something like this.

"Our Father in heaven, bless this couple who soon will be
married. May they live together happily for the rest of their
lives. Help them to love each other more each day, and teach
them to turn to you in prayer in good times and bad times.
In Jesus' name we pray, Amen."

The wedding took place on Saturday, and on Sunday Jackie
wore the same new dress she had worn in the wedding.

"Oh, how pretty," greeted Marilyn at church. "Is that your
wedding dress?"

"No," said Jackie sternly. Marilyn always could say things

that perturbed her. "But it is the dress I wore to the wedding."

"Tell us all about it," pleaded Rachael. So Jackie told about all the pretty clothes, the flowers, and the music.

"What was the best part?" asked Marilyn, for once not making Jackie upset.

"Well the funniest part was when my uncle kissed his new wife," giggled Jackie, "but the best part was when we all marched out of the church. The music and all the smiles made you know you had helped someone do something wonderful."

Story Questions: What was Jackie to be in the wedding? What did the minister say about weddings? What did the minister say in his prayer for the people getting married? What was the funniest part of the wedding? What did Jackie think was the best part? Why?

Scripture Passage: "Husbands, love your wives, even as Christ also loved the church, and gave himself for it" (Eph. 5:25).

Scripture Question: This verse tells husbands they should have great love for their wives. How do you think God wants wives to feel toward husbands?

Scripture Comment for Parents: Much of the fifth and sixth chapters of Ephesians deals with family relationships. Paul, who wrote Ephesians, considered the husband and wife relationship to be as sacred as the relationship between Christ and his church. Christ gave up the glory of heaven in order to come to earth and demonstrate how much he loved us. Likewise, the husband should demonstrate his love for his wife. The wife has no less responsibility to show love to her husband.

Prayer Suggestion: Pray for someone you know who is going to marry soon or who has just recently been married.

Follow-up Activity: Have a pretend wedding. Involve the whole family. Use a sheet for the bride's dress. Cut flower petals from newspaper for the flower girl. Have a ring bearer carry a ring on a pillow. Each family member may need to play several roles to complete the wedding party.

THE FAMILY REUNION

Food Suggestion: Include a favorite food that your family would probably have at a reunion.

Action Activity: Play "Name That Tune." Take turns humming a few bars of a favorite song. See who can guess the song first. The "singer" may need to hum more and more of the song until it is recognized.

Song Time: Include songs sung in the action activity. You may also wish to include "Blest Be the Tie."

Interest Item: Draw a picture of a tree. Be sure to show the various limbs and branches.

Listening Preparation Question: What is a family reunion?

Story: Angela sat curled up in the back of her parents' station wagon. She stared out the window as they drove along, but she was too excited to look at the trees, houses, and farm animals which were alongside the highway. Angela was even too excited to pay attention to the chatter on her father's CB radio. Usually on a trip she would beg her father to let her talk on the CB.

Angela was excited because she was going with her parents to a family reunion. Her mother had explained that a family reunion is when grandparents, parents, aunts, uncles, and cousins all get together at the same time. Angela's excitement began the very moment her mother said "cousins."

Two of Angela's most favorite people in the whole world were her cousins Roger and Polly Beth. Roger was just a little older than Angela, and Polly Beth was just a little younger. The three cousins didn't get to see each other often because Roger and Polly Beth lived in another state, but they always had a lot of fun whenever they were together.

"Are we almost there?" Angela asked eagerly.

"For the tenth time," answered her father sharply, "we still have a little ways to go. You've made the trip to Grandma's house enough to know how much longer it will take." Then a smile broke across his face and he said, "But it's not often that we have a family reunion is it?"

Not too much later Angela's father turned the station wagon into the driveway at Grandmother's house. Several cars were parked in the driveway and alongside the street in front of the house. A long table with a red tablecloth had been set up on the lawn. Angela could see that the table was covered with food. Lawn chairs and benches of all colors and shapes were placed in shady spots under the trees. Angela recognized some of her aunts and uncles, but several of the adults seated in the chairs and standing around the long table did not look familiar. Other than two small babies, she didn't see any children.

No sooner had the station wagon stopped than it seemed that all of the adults surrounded Angela and her parents. Angela didn't even get to put one foot on the ground because one of her uncles picked her up and tossed her into the air, gave her a hug, and then handed her to an aunt. For the next few minutes a very bewildered Angela was passed from one relative to another, and everyone had to kiss or hug her. Angela wished some of the uncles and grown-up cousins had shaved a little closer that morning, and that some of her aunts hadn't used such smelly perfume.

Everyone said something like, "My, how you've grown," "Isn't she pretty," "So you're Angela!" and "Isn't she sweet." Finally someone said, "Don't you want to go play with the other children in the backyard?" and put her down.

Angela was off in a flash. She ran right into Polly Beth and knocked her down. Both girls laughed joyfully as Angela helped her to her feet. Just then Roger ran over and urged the girls to join in the ball game. All the children were playing. Already the family reunion was as exciting as Angela had hoped it would be.

Later the entire group stood in two circles around the long table. The children stood in the inside circle holding hands, and the adults joined hands in the outside circle. Uncle Jerry was the only minister in the family so he always was asked to pray before a meal.

Uncle Jerry prayed, "Dear Father in heaven, we thank you for this time when our family can come together again. We are grateful that our love for one another is strong even though we live far apart. Now, bless this food, and give us all a safe trip back to our homes."

Later that day Angela was back in the station wagon heading toward home. She still paid no attention to the passing scenery or the CB. This time she was thinking about next year's family reunion.

Story Questions: Why was Angela excited? Why didn't she see her favorite cousins often? What happened to Angela when she arrived at her grandmother's house? What did the adults and children do together before they ate? Why do you think the people wanted to come to the family reunion even if it meant traveling a long distance?

Scripture Passage: "I thank my God upon every remembrance of you" (Phil. 1:3).

Scripture Question: Paul wrote this sentence in a letter to friends. What are some possible reasons for Paul thanking God for friends?

Scripture Comment for Parents: Paul was a great distance from his friends in Philippi when he wrote these words. Yet the distance did not diminish his love and appreciation for his friends. The faith they had together in Christ made them like a family. The love of God which draws Christians together overcomes separation by distance and time.

Prayer Suggestion: Pray for a family member who lives far away.

Follow-up Activity: If your family has not done so, make a family tree. You may need to ask grandparents, aunts, and uncles for information on your family history. If the children are old enough, they may wish to write a short biography of some of their relatives. You may wish to place a copy of your family tree in a safe place and continue to add to it in the future.

A New Friend for Ike

Food Suggestion: Dad's choice.

Action Activity: Play "Moving to a New House." Each player says, "I'm moving to a new house and I'm taking a _____." Instead of saying what he is taking, the player must act out the item, such as a toothbrush. In this case the player would pantomime brushing his teeth. The group must guess his item and then go on to the next player who must act out not only his item but all those chosen before him.

Song Time: Include "Holy Bible, Book Divine."

Interest Item: Toy truck or moving van.

Listening Preparation Question: Why did Ike's mother have tears in her eyes?

Story: Ike had his arms crossed and his elbows on the window sill of his upstairs bedroom. He pressed his nose against the window trying to lean forward as far as he could. From his window, Ike could see over the young trees which lined the street in front of his house. He wanted to see down the street as far as he could so he would be the first to see the moving van.

The house next door had been vacant for a long time, but not long ago a new family had bought the house. The new family was supposed to move in today, and Ike was anxiously waiting to see if the family had any children his age.

"I see it! I see it!" he shouted suddenly. "The moving van is coming!" Ike dashed to the hallway and plunged down the stairs, three steps at a time.

"Whoa there," said his mother as he raced toward the kitchen door. "Slow down a bit. The new family has all the help they need. The men from the moving company will unload the truck, and I don't imagine they'd appreciate your getting in their way."

"I won't get in the way, Mom," pleaded Ike. "I'll stay in our yard unless someone asks me to help carry something."

"All right," said his mother, "but just make certain they ask you rather than you asking them."

Once outside Ike positioned himself right in the corner of his yard where he could see all that took place next door, and where anyone could see him if they needed help.

At first only the moving van parked in front of the next-door house. The workmen began unloading the truck, but they did not take anything into the house. Before long a bright blue car parked in front of the moving van.

Ike couldn't believe it when he saw the new family get out of the car. There was a boy just about the same size as Ike. Ike was wondering how he could get the boy's attention when he realized that the boy and his father were walking straight toward him!

"Hello," said the man. "I'm Mr. Norris, and this is my son, Gerald. I wonder if he could stay with you while the men are moving the furniture into the house?"

Ike took Gerald inside to meet his mother, who served them cookies and milk. While they ate, Gerald told Ike and his mother about where he had lived previously, and about all the problems they had getting ready for the move. Gerald made every problem sound funny. Ike's mother had tears in her eyes from laughing so much.

Ike had such a good time showing Gerald his toys and playing games that he forgot all about watching the movers put Gerald's furniture in the house. By the time Mr. Norris came to get Gerald, it seemed to Ike that he had known Gerald all his life. He and Gerald had become the best of friends.

That night just before Ike went to bed, his mother read to him a Bible story about two friends named Jonathan and David. "That was a good story," Ike said to his mother when she finished reading. "I think Gerald and I will be as good friends as were Jonathan and David." Then Ike knelt beside his bed and thanked God for his new friend.

Story Questions: What did Ike want to do to help the new family? What made Ike happy when he saw the new family? Did Ike's mother like the new friend? Why did Ike forget about watching the movers? What are some things you like about your friends? What makes a person a good friend or a best friend? What were the names of the friends in the story Ike's mother read from the Bible?

Scripture Passage: "And Jonathan said to David, Go in peace, forasmuch as we have sworn both of us in the name of the Lord, saying, The Lord be between me and thee, and between my seed and thy seed for ever" (1 Sam. 20:42).

Scripture Question: What did Jonathan mean when he said that the Lord would be between him and David?

Scripture Comment for Parents: Jonathan was the son of King Saul. He was also David's closest friend. Jonathan had protected David at times when Saul was very angry with David. The Bible says Jonathan loved David "as he loved his own soul" (1 Sam. 20:17). When Saul threatened to kill David, Jonathan arranged for David to escape. The verse quoted above was Jonathan's farewell to David. Jonathan was saying that the Lord would keep them friends forever. The best friendships are those based on a mutual belief and commitment to God.

Prayer Suggestion: Pray for your best friend.

Follow-up Activity: Visit a new family in your neighborhood. See if they need help in any way. Invite them to church with you. If you don't know of anyone who has moved near you recently, ask at your school. Your church may have a list of new people who have moved into your community.

ROBIN'S NEW BROTHER

Food Suggestion: Breakfast food.

Action Activity: Dress the baby. Dress a doll or stuffed animal. Include diaper, hat, socks, dress, etc. Time each player to see how long it takes them to dress and undress the baby.

Song Time: Include "How Great Thou Art."

Interest Item: Display an item from your child or children's babyhood.

Listening Preparation Question: What caused Robin to wake up?

Story: "Come on, Robin, let's go for a walk," called Mrs. Alexander.

"I'll be right there, Mother," said Robin, "just as soon as I put Twinkles down for a nap." Twinkles was her favorite doll. Twinkles had soft skin and chubby arms. Robin gently placed Twinkles in a doll crib and covered her with a pink blanket. Then she ran to join her mother.

"Mother," she asked as they started down the street, "Why do you take so many walks? You go walking once or twice a day now, and before you never took any walks."

Mrs. Alexander looked down at her daughter and smiled, "I walk a lot now because the doctor told me to do it. He said I needed the exercise to get ready for when the baby is born."

"Is the baby really in your tummy, Mother?" asked Robin.

"Not inside my stomach, Robin, but in a special place inside my body. A place God made just for babies," said Mother. "Sometimes I can feel the baby kicking."

"But Liz told me that babies came from the hospital," said Robin.

"Most babies are born in a hospital," replied Mrs. Alexander. "But that's because the mothers go there so doctors and nurses can take care of them and the new babies."

"Will you have to go to the hospital when our baby is born?" asked Robin as she skipped over a pothole in the road.

"Yes, I will," was the reply.

"But I don't want you to go. I want you to stay with me and let the baby be born at home," said Robin, with a slight quiver of her chin.

Mrs. Alexander put her arm around Robin and gave her a hug, "I know you do," she said, "but Aunt Sue will take care of you while I am gone. And besides both the baby and I will be better off with the care they can give at the hospital."

"Does it hurt to have a baby?" asked Robin.

"It is uncomfortable," said her mother, "but exercising like we are doing now helps, and the doctors do all they can to make you comfortable. But Robin, the discomfort is nothing to compare with the joy of having a new person in our home. We will always be thankful to God both for you and the new baby. Now let's head back home," said Mother. "I think we have had enough walking for today."

"And I need to wake my Twinkles baby from her nap," said Robin, as she skipped ahead of her mother.

A few days later Robin was awakened early in the morning by the telephone ringing. She rubbed her eyes and walked into the kitchen. She was surprised to see Aunt Sue talking on the phone. Her mother and father were nowhere around.

"Good morning, Robin," said Aunt Sue cheerfully. "This is your father on the telephone, and he has something he wants to tell you."

Robin was still too sleepy to realize what was going on. She really woke up though when she heard her father say, "Robin, you have a new baby brother, and his name is Chris!"

Robin thought the days would never pass before her mother and Chris could come home. Finally, one morning Robin's father said, "Let's go get your Mother and new brother."

Robin waited eagerly in the car at the front door of the hospital. Then she saw a nurse pushing a wheelchair toward the car. In the wheelchair was her mother and in her mother's arms was a baby wrapped in a blue blanket. When her mother pulled back the blanket, Robin touched Chris and exclaimed, "His skin is softer than Twinkles!" And she knew that she, too, would always be thankful to God for her new brother.

Story Questions: Why did Mrs. Alexander walk so much? Why are most babies born in a hospital? What did Robin's father tell her on the telephone? What did Robin think about her new brother?

Scripture Passage: "Lo, children are an heritage of the Lord" (Ps. 127:3).

Scripture Question: This verse says that children are a

blessing for parents. Who does the verse say gives children to parents?

Scripture Comment for Parents: This verse reminds parents that their children actually were given to them by God. Each child is a precious treasure of priceless value. Of all the earthly blessings God bestows, there is no greater blessing than that of a child. Each child is unique and holy unto God. The birth of a child is a time for rejoicing and celebration because God has greatly increased the spiritual richness of a family.

Prayer Suggestion: Give thanks for each member of the family, beginning with the youngest.

Follow-up Activity: You may wish to use this time to answer questions about where babies come from. Some children have fears which they have difficulty expressing, such as fear of the baby being hurt while in the womb. This could be explained by placing a small object in a plastic bag filled with water to show them how the baby is protected in the womb. Use as many visual illustrations as possible.

If you do not feel comfortable discussing this topic with your child, then perhaps you could read together one of the many good books available on the subject.

Seasons and Holidays

Spring
PLANNING A GARDEN

Food Suggestion: Include fresh fruit or fresh vegetables in your snack time.

Action Activity: Play and sing "Farmer in the Dell," or act out the story of Peter Rabbit in Mr. McGregor's garden.

Song Time: Include "For the Beauty of the Earth."

Interest Item: A seed catalog or a fresh vegetable.

Listening Preparation Question: What happened to Seth's tomato plant?

Story: Seth stood looking out the window, his nose pressed to the glass. "Rain again today," he said to himself. The weatherman said that April showers would bring May flowers, but Seth didn't care. He just wished it would stop. "Today will be boring," he thought.

Just then the phone rang. "It's for you, Seth," called Mother.

"Hi, Seth, it's Granddaddy. Why don't you get your mother to bring you over and you can help me plant my garden."

"But we can't plant a garden today," said Seth. "It's raining!"

Granddaddy chuckled, "We will plant it on paper today, Seth. I have to figure out what we want and order the seeds. Thought you might like to help."

"OK," said Seth, "I'll be over."

Seth and his grandfather looked through the seed catalog. There was a lot to do because Granddaddy always had a big vegetable garden as well as the prettiest flower garden in the whole county.

"Do we have to plant cabbage this year, Granddaddy?" asked Seth, making a face. "I don't like cabbage!"

"Maybe not as much cabbage this year, but your grandmother likes to make fresh cabbage slaw, and I like to eat it," said Granddaddy.

"How do you decide what to plant where?" asked Seth.

"Some fruit and vegetables need lots of sun, and others need some shade. Some plants need more water than others," said Granddaddy, "and so we plant them in areas that stay damp longer."

"Why does God make it rain, Granddaddy?" asked Seth looking out the window.

"Why if we didn't have water on the earth, all living things would die. Remember the little flowerpot with a tomato plant in it that I gave you last year," said Granddaddy. "It looked so pretty and was beginning to bloom until you forgot to water it. What happened?"

"It shriveled up and looked sick," said Seth, looking down at his toes. "But then I remembered and gave it some water.

Then Daddy planted it outside and we had lots of tomatoes!"

"See, it would have died without water, and so would all living things. Rain is God's way of giving the earth a drink," said Granddaddy.

"God knows just what we need, doesn't he?" replied Seth.

"He most certainly does," answered Granddaddy.

Story Questions: Why did Seth think the day would be boring? What did his grandfather want him to do? What kind of books did they look at? How did Seth's grandfather decide where to plant seeds? How does God give the earth a drink?

Scripture Passage: "Then I will give you rain in due season, and the land shall yield her increase, and the trees of the field shall yield their fruit" (Lev. 26:4).

Scripture Question: What does the rain have to do with the food we eat?

Scripture Comment for Parents: God promised the Israelites that if they would keep his laws, he would provide them rain at the appropriate times to make their crops grow. God still controls the elements and provides the mixture of rain and sunshine needed for our food supply.

Prayer Suggestion: Give thanks to God for the fruit and vegetables you eat. Thank him also for the rain and sunshine.

Follow-up Activity: If you have a seed catalog, look through it. Or make an outline map of your yard and consider where flowers would look nice and would grow well.

Summer
SUMMER STARS

Food Suggestion: Cake and Kool-aid.

Action Activity: If time, season, and location permit, go outside and catch lightning bugs. If not, do exercises such as jumping jacks, sit-ups, and push-ups.

Song Time: Include "Heavenly Sunlight."

Interest Item: Make several pinpricks in a piece of dark blue construction paper. Wrap the paper around a small lamp so that the light comes through the pinholes. Make sure the paper does not touch the light bulb.

Listening Preparation Question: When do stars twinkle?

Story: Mrs. Horton was putting the last spoonful of icing on a cake when the kitchen door burst open suddenly. Cindy and Mindy began calling, "Hey, Mom!" as soon as the door swung open. They did not see their mother at the table until they were almost all the way through the kitchen.

"Oh, there you are, Mom," said both of the twins at the same time. "Can we go over to Beverly's house tonight? Can we please? Say yes. Say yes, please." And then each girl in her own way tried to explain why it was so important to go to Beverly's house.

"Just a minute, please!" said their mother, "I can't understand you both at once. Why don't you sit down and cool off with some lemonade and cake while you take turns talking. You are perspiring so much it looks like you ran all the way home from Vacation Bible School."

"We did, Mom," said Mindy, as she climbed into a chair, "because we want to know if we can go to Beverly's house tonight. She invited us to come."

"But Beverly's much older than you. Didn't you tell me that she is a junior assistant in Bible School this year?" inquired the twins' mother.

"Yes," replied Cindy, "She helps our teacher during play time, and she stays with us during story time."

"Well, why did she invite you to her house at night?" asked their mother.

Again both girls started talking at the same time, but finally Mindy said, "You tell her, Cindy."

"Today," began Cindy, "we studied about how God made the earth and the sun and the stars. Beverly told us that her Girl Scout troop had studied a lot about stars, and if we'd come to her house after dark when the stars are out, she'd teach us some things about stars."

Mindy chimed in, "Beverly told us that actually the stars are twinkling right now, but we can't see them because of the bright sun."

Later that evening the twins' mother walked with the girls to Beverly's house. While the mothers talked inside, Beverly took Cindy and Mindy out in the backyard. For a few minutes all three girls tried catching lightning bugs.

"Now let's lay down in the grass and look up into the sky," said Beverly.

"Boy, you certainly can see more stars at night than you can during the daytime!" exclaimed Mindy. "In fact, I don't think I've ever seen a daytime star."

"Oh yes you have," laughed Beverly. "You see one every day that the sun shines, because the sun is a star also."

"Wow!" whispered Cindy, "but why is it so much bigger than all the other stars?"

"The sun is the only star close enough to the earth to look like a ball. All the other stars are so far away that they look like tiny spots of light," explained Beverly.

"That's a long, long way," said Cindy as she gazed upward into the dark velvet sky which seemed to be sprinkled with tiny diamonds.

"Right above us is a group of stars called 'The Big Dipper,' " commented Beverly.

"Why are they called that?" asked Cindy.

"Because if you could draw a line from one star to another," said Beverly, "it would look like a cup with a long handle on it."

Beverly told the girls many things about stars before their mother said that it was time to go. On the way home they told their mother all they could remember. Mindy looked up at the sky one more time before they went into the house. "God certainly made everything beautiful, didn't he?" she said.

"And big, too," said Cindy.

Story Questions: Where had the twins been? What had they been studying in Vacation Bible School? What did they learn about the sun? What did the stars look like to the girls? How big are stars? How close are the stars to each other?

Scripture Passage: "And God made two great lights: the greater light to rule the day, and the lesser light to rule the night: he made the stars also" (Gen. 1:16).

Scripture Question: What were the two great lights God made?

Scripture Comment for Parents: Creation of the world was a magnificent event. We are awed at God's power when we realize all that he did in creating the world. Yet the more we learn about the universe, we realize that the greatness of God is far, far more than we can ever understand. New space discoveries by astronomers and astronauts should make us intensely aware that "he made the stars also," is not just an incidental statement. We can say with the psalmist, "And the heavens shall praise thy wonders, O Lord" (Ps. 89:5).

Prayer Suggestion: Pray a prayer of praise to God for all of his beautiful creation.

Follow-up Activity: If at all possible, go out and look at the stars. With the help of an encyclopedia or astronomy book, see if you can find the Big Dipper and the Milky Way.

Fall
THE LEAF HOUSE

Food Suggestion: Gingerbread men.

Action Activity: Let each child take turns driving a nail into a board. Be sure the wood is thicker than the nails are long!

Song Time: Include "How Firm a Foundation."

Interest Item: A pile of index cards and a rock.

Listening Preparation Question: What happened to the leaf house?

Story: "I love to play in the leaves," said Scott. "I think fall is my very favorite season."

"Let's get some rakes and make a leaf house," said Dana.

"A leaf house!" exclaimed Scott and Mitzi, "What is that?"

"I'll show you," shouted Dana, as she ran home to get her rake. "Just go get a rake."

Soon all three children were back in Scott's front yard. "Are we going to pile the leaves real high and then tunnel into them?" asked Scott. "I think that would be a great house!"

"No," said Dana mysteriously, "just make several piles sort of close together."

The children worked quickly and soon had six piles of leaves. "Now," said Dana, "let's make an outline of rooms with our leaves. I am in the kitchen. Scott, you make the living room. Mitzi, you make the baby's room."

"Say, this looks neat," said Scott. "I'll ask my mother if she will make us some sandwiches and we can have lunch in our leaf house kitchen."

"Fine," said Dana, "and while you are gone, Mitzi and I will make some more bedrooms and a den."

"Where is the kitchen door?" asked Scott coming back from his house. His hands were full of food.

"Oh! I forgot," said Dana. "Here, I'll make one," and at that she raked open a door in the wall of leaves.

"Let's play this again tomorrow," said Mitzi as the children finished their lunch. "Maybe my Mom will let me make gingerbread men."

That night there was a bad storm. The wind howled and the rain poured down. The next morning when the children went out to play there was nothing left of their leaf house but a few piles of wet soggy leaves.

"I guess we can't play in our house again," said Scott, looking very sad.

"What am I going to do with our gingerbread men?" asked Mitzi.

"I know," replied the others, "let's eat them!"

As the children stood in the wet grass munching their gingerbread, Dana said, "You know, our leaf house is sort of like the Bible story we had in Sunday School last week."

"You mean about the house on the sand?" asked Scott. "But we built our house on the grass."

"I know," said Dana, "but the wind and rain came, and the house was lost."

"Then our real houses must be like the house built on the rock," said Scott, looking at all the houses down the street.

"Hey, that's right," said Dana, "and we'd be smarter to play inside than here in this wet grass and leaves."

As they headed toward Scott's house, Dana said, "But don't forget the teacher said that the real wisdom in that Sunday School lesson was in choosing to follow Jesus."

Story Questions: How do you make a leaf house? What did the storm do to the leaf house? Can you tell anything about the two houses the children had studied in Sunday School? Which of the two was like the leaf house?

Scripture Passage: "Therefore whosoever heareth these sayings of mine and doeth them, I will liken him unto a wise man, which built his house upon a rock" (Matt. 7:24).

Scripture Question: Why would a person be considered wise if he obeyed or followed Jesus' teaching?

Scripture Comments for Parents: Some people refuse to hear the teachings of Jesus. Therefore, the first step toward salvation is to hear (read or listen to) the Word of God. The second step is to obey or follow the teachings. Hearing the teachings is not enough. We must demonstrate our faith by living out the teachings. We can build our lives upon the rock of the Scriptures without any fear that the teachings will be proven in error.

Prayer Suggestion: Pray for personal discipline in Bible study to learn and live the teachings of Christ.

Follow-up Activity: Make two houses of index cards. Use ten cards for each house. Make one house with cards only. Tape the other card house together. Blow on the houses to see what happens.

Winter
As Special As a Snowflake

Food Suggestion: Ice cream.

Action Activity: Have a snowball fight, using wadded up paper for the snowballs.

Song Time: Include such songs about nature as "God's Beautiful World."

Interest Item: Picture of a snow scene.

Listening Preparation Question: What shape is a snowflake?

Story: Mary Beth and Billy jumped for joy as they ran from the school bus stop. It was snowing! Big flakes fell on their jackets and stayed there for a minute before melting away. Already the ground was covered with a thin layer of white.

"No school tomorrow if this keeps up" cheered Billy as he tried to catch a snowflake on his tongue.

All evening the snow continued. "Millions and trillions of snowflakes" murmured Billy as he watched the snow coming down.

"Children, did you know that no two snowflakes are exactly alike?" said Mother.

"Are some square and some round?" asked Mary Beth.

"No," said Mother, "each snowflake has six points, but each has a different feather-like design."

"Why?" asked Billy.

"Snow is really a little droplet of moisture that freezes on its way to the ground. When it freezes that is the shape it takes," answered Mother. "You know, God has so arranged nature that each snowflake is different."

"Not really so different if they all have six points," said Mary Beth.

"Different and yet alike," answered Mother. "You and Billy both have two arms, two legs, a head, and a body. Yet, you are different aren't you?"

"Of course we are different. She's a girl and I'm a boy," pronounced Billy.

"But you don't look like your cousin Joe either," said Mother. "God has made each of us alike and yet each of us is different. There is no one else in the whole world just exactly like us. No one at all. And that makes each of us special."

Story Questions: What shape is a snowflake? How is a snowflake formed? Who makes the snowflake? How were Billy and Mary Beth like the snowflakes? What made Billy and Mary Beth special? How are you special?

Scripture Passage: "But the very hairs of your head are all numbered" (Matt. 10:30).

Scripture Question: What does this verse teach us about each person being special?

Scripture Comment for Parents: This verse illustrates how much God knows and cares for us individually. We will not find a number written on each hair, but we can be assured that God has a personal concern for each of us. God knows more about us than we know about ourselves. He knows more about us because he created us. In God's sight, each of us are as different and as special as a snowflake.

Prayer Suggestion: Name some family friends who are of different ages and races. Thank God for making each person different and for caring for each person.

Follow-up Activity: Cut out large paper snowflakes. Put favorite Scripture verses on each. Hang in the child's bedroom.

New Year's Day
THE NEW YEAR'S RESOLUTION

Food Suggestion: Popcorn balls.

Action Activity: Make a clean sweep for the new year. Spend fifteen minutes sweeping and dusting and picking up throughout the house.

Song Time: Include "The Old Rugged Cross."

Interest Item: A bell to ring in the new year.

Listening Preparation Question: What made Darrel's resolution more important?

Story: "Hey, Mom!" yelled Maria at the top of her voice as she jumped over the last step coming down the stairs.

"You needn't yell, I'm right here beside you," said her mother sternly, as she stepped from the hall closet where she had been hanging up coats.

Maria was so startled by the sudden appearance from the closet that she jumped straight up in the air. "Oh, Mom, you scared me," she said. "I didn't know you were there."

"I knew where you were Maria," her mother replied, still speaking sternly. "You simply must learn not to yell in the house. Now, what do you want?"

"Mom, what is a resolution?" asked Maria.

"There are different kinds of resolutions, but I imagine you are talking about New Year's resolutions," said her mother.

"Yes, that's it. Darrel is up in his room writing his New Year's resolutions, but he won't tell me what they are!"

Just then Darrel came down the stairs. "I tried to explain to her, Mom," said Darrel, "but I guess I didn't do too good of a job. Besides, she was more interested in trying to see what I had written than in listening to what I was saying."

"I do hope your resolutions include hanging up your own clothes. I've spent the last fifteen minutes hanging up coats and jackets owned by every member of our family," said his mother.

"Would someone please tell me what is a New Year's resolution?" pleaded Maria.

"A New Year's resolution," said their mother, as she sat down on the bottom step," is sort of a promise you make to yourself."

"What kind of promise?" asked Maria, as she and Darrel sat on the floor in front of their mother.

"Let me try again," said Darrel. "New Year's day is a time for thinking back over the year past and remembering some things you could have done better or maybe even remembering some things you should not have done. Then you make a resolution that next year you'll do better."

"I understand," said Maria, "and you may also promise yourself not to do some things."

"That's right," said her mother, "like promising yourself not to yell in the house."

"Oh!" said Maria. Then she asked, "Is New Year's Day a church day, Mom?"

"Some churches do have special services," said her mother, "either on New Year's Day or the night before, but the day is not a religious holiday. However, in Old Testament times there was a special holiday which marked the beginning of a new year with God."

"Did they call it New Year's Day?" asked Maria.

"No," replied her mother, "they called it the Day of Atonement. It was a day all of the people of Israel asked God for forgiveness of their sins."

Darrel suddenly sat straight up and exclaimed, "They could have called it a Day of Resolutions also. They must have thought back over the sins they had committed the past year and promised to live better lives the next year."

"Perhaps so," replied his mother. "And perhaps we need to think of ways we can live better for God next year."

"I have an idea," said Maria. "Tonight when we have family worship, let's ask God to forgive our sins for the past year. And then let each person in the family share their resolutions for next year."

"That is a good idea," said her mother. "Let's go find some paper to write our resolutions."

"I think I need to do some more work on mine," said Darrel as he started back up the stairs. "They'll be more important if I make promises to God instead of just to myself."

Story Questions: What scared Maria? Why was she looking for her mother? What are New Year's resolutions? What were the two resolutions suggested by the mother? How was the Day of Atonement like New Year's Day? What did Darrel suggest as another name for the Day of Atonement? What was Maria's suggestion for family worship?

Scripture Passage: "And this shall be an everlasting statute unto you, to make an atonement for the children of Israel for all their sins once a year" (Lev. 16:34).

Scripture Question: How long did God expect people to keep on asking forgiveness for their sins?

Scripture Comment for Parents: The word *atonement* is the English translation of a Hebrew word which means "cover" or "covering." Therefore, atonement implies that our sins are covered. The phrase *children of Israel* refers to all the people of Israel—both children and adults. Parents may be interested in reading the entire sixteenth chapter of Leviticus to learn the origin of the term *scapegoat.*

Prayer Suggestion: Pray for the entire family, asking forgiveness for sins of the past year, and asking that each member will walk closer to God during the next year.

Follow-up Activity: Write New Year's resolutions both individually and as a family. You may wish to tape-record your resolutions and keep them to serve both as a reminder and to have a record of the children's voices from year to year.

Valentine's Day
THE LOPSIDED VALENTINE

Food Suggestion: Heart-shaped cookies.

Action Activity: Cut out a number of paper hearts. Hide them around the room. The person who collects the most hearts wins a kiss from each family member.

Song Time: Include "Jesus Loves Me."

Interest Item: Box of valentine cards.

Listening Preparation Question: Why was Joanna good at making valentines?

Story: "May I go over to Joanna's house and make valentines?" asked Alice.

"Be sure you are home by five o'clock. And, Alice, you can take those white paper doilies if you want," said mother.

"Thanks," said Alice, running out the door.

Joanna had construction paper, glue, tape, ribbon, and some cute heart stickers spread out on the dining room table when Alice arrived.

"This is going to be fun," Joanna said. "I just love making valentines."

"Whose are you going to make first?" asked Alice.

"I think I'll make one for my teacher, and then one for my mother. I'm not sure after that," said Joanna.

"I think I'll make one for my teacher, and then one for each of my two grandmothers," volunteered Alice.

The girls started to work. Alice took a piece of red construction paper and folded it to cut out a heart.

Joanna giggled, "You certainly have a fat valentine."

Alice folded the valentine again and cut off some of the sides. "Now," she sighed, "it's too skinny." She looked over at Joanna's paper heart. It was perfect—not too big or too small.

"I think I'll try again," she said, picking up another piece of paper. This time she cut very carefully. "I hope this will do," she said looking questioningly at the paper. "Have you ever made valentines before?" Alice asked Joanna.

"Oh yes, I do it every year," Joanna replied.

"I guess I just need practice then," said Alice, trying to stick the white lacy doily to the red heart.

Both girls worked quietly. Every now and then Alice would look at the beautiful valentine Joanna was making. She would sigh and keep on working. The afternoon passed quickly and soon it was time to go.

As the girls were cleaning up their work, Alice said to Joanna, "I wish my valentines were half as nice as yours. But thank you for inviting me."

Alice walked home very slowly. The more she looked at her valentines, the uglier they seemed.

"Did you have a nice time?" asked Mother.

"Yes, Mother," said Alice.

"Then why the long face?"

"Oh Mother, you should see Joanna's valentines. They are so pretty, and mine are lopsided and have sticky glue all over them."

"Why do we send valentines, Alice?" asked her mother.

"To tell people that we love them," said Alice, her chin quivering.

"Did you work hard to make your valentines?" asked Mother.

Alice nodded her head very fast.

"The people who receive your valentines love you also," said Mother. "They will know how much effort went into the valentines, and they will be so happy that you took the time to show your love for them. No one cares if your valentines aren't perfect, or not even as good as Joanna's. The fact that you made them is what is important."

Story Questions: Why did Alice go to Joanna's house? What did Joanna have on the dining room table? What happened to Alice's first valentine? Why was Alice sad when she went home? What did Alice's mother tell her?

Scripture Passage: "And be ye kind one to another" (Eph. 4:32).

Scripture Question: What are some ways of being kind?

Scripture Comment: Valentine's Day is not a religious event, but the exchange of valentine cards and gifts does express the intent of this verse. The full verse calls for acts of kindness toward other people. The giving of valentines, whether they be homemade or bought, is one means of sharing kindness.

Prayer Suggestion: Name two or three people who have made a special effort to be kind to you. Give thanks to God for those people.

Follow-up Activity: Make valentines.

Easter
THE FATHER-SON CAMPOUT

Food Suggestion: Eggs and bacon.

Action Activity: Play a motion game. Have the family

sit on the floor in a circle. First player makes a movement such as swinging his arms. The next player makes that motion and adds one of his own. Continue around the circle with each player adding a new motion.

Song Time: Include "Low in the Grave He Lay" or "Because He Lives."

Interest Item: A flower.

Listening Preparation Question: Why did David sleep in his clothes?

Story: "Hey, wake up sleepyhead," said Mr. Mason. "We've got to pack these sleeping bags before breakfast." David slowly opened his eyes and reluctantly peered out from within the sleeping bag.

"But it's cold outside the sleeping bag, Dad," said David.

"You'll warm up once you get moving around," answered David's father. "And besides, everyone else in our tent is already outside."

David jumped out of his sleeping bag and quickly put on his shoes. He didn't need to get dressed because he had slept in his clothes in order to stay warm. Mr. Mason helped David roll up his sleeping bag, and then they stepped outside of the tent.

Other tents were set up alongside theirs, and a campfire was burning in front of the middle tent. David's church had sponsored a father-son campout, and most of the boys in David's Sunday School class had come.

Breakfast was cooked over the campfire, and David had never eaten such delicious eggs and bacon. It seemed that the cool morning air made him extra hungry.

After breakfast the camp leader, Mr. Neely, asked all the men and boys to gather in a circle around the campfire. Then he said, "In a few minutes we want each father and son to go off together to someplace out in the woods. We want you to spend some time talking and praying together." Then he dismissed the group.

David and his father walked up the hill behind the tents. Soon they could not see any of the other fathers and sons.

"Let's sit here on top of the hill," said Mr. Mason. The two talked about home and church and friends. Then Mr. Mason took out his pocket New Testament and read a verse to David. After a few more minutes of talking about the verse of Scripture Mr. Mason asked David to pray, and then Mr. Mason prayed. Mr. Mason ended his prayer by saying, "And thank you for sending Jesus to die for us."

When his father stopped praying, David asked, "Why did Jesus have to die?"

"That's a good question, David," said Mr. Mason. "Jesus died to show us how much he loved us and to save us from our sins. But remember that Jesus did not stay dead."

"Oh, I know," said David, "He comes alive again each Easter."

"That's not exactly correct, David," said Mr. Mason. "Jesus is alive all the time."

"But every Easter we talk and sing about him coming alive on that day," responded David.

"Yes," said Mr. Mason, "But what we are doing is celebrating the fact that after he was killed, he came back to life, and he stayed alive."

"I don't understand," said David.

"David," Mr. Mason replied, "each year we celebrate your birthday. That means once each year on a special day we give thanks that you were born. But you are not born each birthday. You are living all the time between birthday celebrations."

"Oh, now I see," said David, "Jesus is alive all the time, but Easter is the special time each year when we give thanks for the time he came back from the dead. Right, Dad?" asked David.

"Right, Son," said Mr. Mason, as they headed back down the hill toward the tents.

Story Questions: Where had David slept? Where was breakfast prepared? What did the fathers and sons do after breakfast? What did Mr. Mason say at the close of his prayer? Can you explain what happened to Jesus after he was crucified?

Scripture Passage: "Go quickly, and tell his disciples that he is risen from the dead" (Matt. 28:7).

Scripture Question: Who was the person who had risen from the dead?

Scripture Comment for Parents: The Gospel of Matthew states that two women first discovered Jesus' resurrection from the dead. An angel greeted them at the tomb and showed them that Jesus was no longer there. The angel gave the women the assignment to tell the disciples. They were to go quickly, and tell. This same good news is ours to share with other potential disciples, and it is of such importance that we should share it with others as quickly as possible.

Prayer Suggestion: Pray for at least two people you know who have not accepted Jesus as their Savior.

Follow-up Activity: Plant flowers. Explain to the children that only when the seed is buried can it bring forth life.

Independence Day
THE PICNIC

Food Suggestion: Hot dogs or apple pie.

Action Activity: Have your own Fourth of July parade. Pots and spoons make fine instruments. March around the house. Take turns being the leader of the band.

Song Time: Include "America, the Beautiful."

Interest Item: A copy of the Declaration of Independence.

Listening Preparation Question: Why do we still celebrate Independence Day?

Story: "The pastor said we were going to have a church picnic on In-de-pen-dence Day." said Paul. "What is that?"

"Why that's the Fourth of July," his brother, Jay, answered. "When did the pastor tell you that?"

"He came into our choir and asked Mrs. Barnes if we could sing 'America' for the In-de-pen-dence Day picnic," replied Paul.

"That is great," said Jay, "now I can see my church friends for a whole day."

"What else is going to happen at the picnic?" asked Mother.

"I think the Scouts are going to bring flags and someone is going to speak," answered Paul.

"Sounds like an old-fashioned Fourth of July," said Mother. I'll have to see if there is a food committee and find out what we should bring."

"But no one has answered my question yet!" said Paul. "What is Independence Day—Fourth of July? Why are we having a picnic?"

"Many years ago," said Mother, "in 1776 on the fourth day of July, some of our country's leaders got together and declared our independence from Great Britain. That's why we call it Independence Day."

"But why do we celebrate it today? It's been a long time since 1776," questioned Paul.

"We celebrate your birthday, don't we?" asked Mother.

"Sure!" said Paul.

"In the same way we celebrate the birthday of our country," answered Mother.

"I hope there will be fireworks," said Jay. "I love fireworks!"

"I'm sure there will be," said Mother.

"Why fireworks?" asked Paul.

"Because we always have it!" said Jay, getting somewhat disgusted.

"No, there must be a better answer," said Mother, taking a book from the bookcase. "Let's look it up in the encyclopedia. Here it is, this is the answer. John Adams, our second president, said he hoped the day would always be celebrated with 'illuminations,' which is what he called fireworks, and games, and parades."

"I guess President Adams thought it should be a day for doing fun things," said Jay.

"Yes," said Mother, as she continued reading the encyclopedia, "and also he said that 'the day ought to be commemorated as the day of deliverance, by solomn acts of devotion to God Almighty.'"

"What did he mean by 'day of deliverance'?" asked Jay.

Mother replied, "He meant that the Fourth of July was the day our country declared freedom from control by another country."

"I wish they had called it Freedom Day. That's much easier to say than In-de-pen-dence Day," said Paul.

"I have to admit that I'm glad you asked all those questions," said Jay. "I never did understand why we had a worship service at the end of the Fourth of July picnic. Now I know we have the service in order to thank God for our freedom."

Story Questions: How did Paul and Jay's church plan to celebrate Independence Day? What were some of the things that would take place at the picnic? What is Independence Day? What President began the Independence Day celebration? Why was a worship service planned as part of the picnic?

Scripture Passage: "Blessed is the nation whose God is the Lord" (Ps. 33:12).

Scripture Question: Why would a nation be blessed if all its people obeyed God?

Scripture Comment for Parents: A nation may make an official proclamation about trust in God, but the proclamation is worthless unless the people of that nation truly worship him. Worship cannot be legislated. It must be a natural response from trusting in God. Families all across the country, rather than government officials, will determine whether or not our nation genuinely believes "In God we trust."

Prayer Suggestion: Pray that each member of the family will do all they can to make our nation a God-led nation.

Follow-up Activity: Make American and Christian flags out of construction paper. Display in each child's room.

Halloween
HALLOWEEN CANDY

Food Suggestion: Doughnuts and hot chocolate.

Action Activity: Play "Pin the Nose on the Pumpkin." Cut a large pumpkin out of newspaper and make noses out of construction paper. Blindfold each player and let each one try to place the nose in the middle of the pumpkin.

Song Time: Children may wish to sing Halloween songs learned at school.

Interest Item: Jack-o'-lantern.

Listening Preparation Question: Who is the ghost in this story?

Story: Gina was so excited that she couldn't eat her supper. This was Halloween, and she and her best friend, Lucy, were going to go trick-or-treating by themselves.

"Now you be sure to go only to the houses where you know the people," said Mother. "And watch carefully when you cross the street."

"Oh, I will, Mother," Gina said, tripping over her costume.

"I'm not so certain that being a ghost was such a good idea. Are you sure you can see?" asked Mother.

"Yes, Mom," said Gina, going out the door.

"Lucy, is that you?" giggled Gina, almost falling down the steps.

"Yes," said Lucy. "I borrowed my cousin's football suit, and the blood is really red ink."

"Where do you want to go first?" asked Gina.

"Let's go down your side of the street and then back up by my house," answered Lucy.

The girls stopped at several houses. "We must be the first ones out tonight," said Gina. "Everyone certainly is giving us a lot of candy."

Lucy agreed and then said, "The Curry's house is next. They have a light on over the front door, but it doesn't look like they are at home. Their car is not even in the driveway." Then Lucy exclaimed, "I see a note on the door. Let's go see what it says," and she hurried up the walk.

The note read: "We had to leave home tonight, but we wanted to share Halloween with you. Take one candy bar and leave the rest for those who come after you. Thank you, Mrs. Curry."

"That was nice of them," said Gina. "Hey Lucy, you just took three candy bars!"

"I know," said Lucy, "but the Curry's won't know, and if we don't take it, someone else will. In fact, here come those Price boys now. You know how mean they are. They probably will take the whole bowl."

Gina was scared. She didn't know what to do. Should she:

—Take several bars of candy?

—Take only what the note said to take?

—Take it all and share with the other children in the neighborhood later so that the Price boys would not get it?

Story Questions: Why were Gina and Lucy in costume? What was different at the Curry's house? What did the note from Mrs. Curry tell them? Why did Lucy say it was OK to take more than one candy bar? Discuss the three questions Gina asked herself. Which should she do? Why?

Scripture Passage: "Now I pray to God that ye do no evil; . . . but that ye should do that which is honest" (2 Cor. 13:7).

Scripture Question: What does it mean to be honest?

Scripture Comment for Parents: This verse comes from one of Paul's letters to an early Christian church. Paul urged the Christians to be honest in what they did. They were to keep from doing anything which might be considered evil or wrong.

Prayer Suggestion: Ask God to help you know the difference between evil and honesty, and to do that which is honest.

Follow-up Activity: Make Halloween decorations.

Thanksgiving
TURKEY DAY

Food Suggestion: Some food from the traditional Thanksgiving meal.

Action Activity: Each family member is given a feather. At a given signal each person blows his feather into the air.

The person who can keep the feather up the longest without the feather touching the floor is the winner.

Song Time: Include such Thanksgiving songs as "Come, Ye Thankful People, Come."

Interest Item: Picture of a Pilgrim.

Listening Preparation Question: What is the correct name for Turkey Day?

Story: "Next Thursday is Turkey Day, and we don't have to go to school," said Paul.

"Turkey Day!" said Jason. "What is that?"

"Oh, its just a day we stay home and watch parades and football on television and eat turkey," replied Paul.

"I know what you are talking about now," said Jason, "only it's called Thanksgiving."

"Why call it that?" asked Paul.

"Because many years ago the Pilgrims started Thanksgiving Day. Don't you remember that at school we cut out the pictures of people in funny black hats? Mrs. Barry's fourth grade had a play with Indians and Pilgrims."

"Oh, yeah, now I remember," said Paul. "But what did they have to be thankful about?"

"The Pilgrims had a hard time, and a lot of people died during their first winter in the new world," answered Jason. "But by the next summer things were better. They had grown some corn and other food, and had built better houses. The Pilgrims knew that the following winter they would not go hungry. They felt so happy and thankful that they decided to have a big celebration and invite the Indians who had helped them."

"So, what does that have to do with us?" asked Paul.

"We still have reasons to be thankful," said Jason. "Just think about food, clothing, houses, and all the things we have."

Paul then inquired, "The Pilgrims had the Indians to thank, but who do we thank?"

Jason replied, "The Pilgrims were thankful that the Indians helped them. But most of all they were thankful to God for giving them the strength to continue."

"Thanksgiving Day today," Jason continued, "is a time for us to thank those who have helped us through the year. But most of all this is the day we should praise and thank God for all that he has given to us."

"I guess it is more than just a turkey day," said Paul.

"It sure is," answered Jason.

Story Questions: Who started Thanksgiving Day? Why were the Pilgrims thankful? Why was Jason thankful? Why were the Pilgrims thankful to God? What should we do on Thanksgiving Day?

Scripture Passage: "Enter into his gates with thanksgiving, and into his courts with praise: be thankful unto him, and bless his name" (Ps. 100:4).

Scripture Question: Do you think this verse tells us to say thank you to God just one time, to not say thank you aloud, or to continually say thank you to God?

Scripture Comment for Parents: This verse comes from a short psalm which suggests that any thanksgiving to God should be a festive, joyful occasion. Special emphasis is placed on repeated expression of thanks when we enter into God's house.

Prayer Suggestion: List specific people for whom to give thanks. Include people not in the immediate family or circle of friends. When making the list, specify why you are thankful for each one.

Follow-up Activity: Write a thank-you note to someone who has helped your family this year. Small children can draw pictures to illustrate their feelings.

Christmas
THE WISE MAN'S SMILE

Food Suggestion: Christmas cookies.

Action Activity: "Cotton Ball Game." Place two bowls on a table. Fill one bowl with cotton balls. Blindfold a family member who attempts to move the balls from one bowl to the other, using only a spoon. The person who moves the most balls wins.

Song Time: Christmas carols. Include "We Three Kings of Orient Are."

Interest Item: Nativity scene picture or figurines.

Listening Preparation Question: Why did Troy cry while looking at the Christmas tree?

Story: Troy sat staring at the Christmas tree. Through his tears the lights even looked more shiny. The Nativity scene in front of the tree seemed even more alive.

"I don't want to share my new presents with those Jackson children," he thought. "I'm sorry that their tree caught on fire and burned all of their new things, but these are mine," he said stubbornly to himself. "Maybe Mother will let me give some of my old toys to those kids." Then slumping down further he sighed, "No, I don't think she would let me do that."

Troy continued to sit gazing at the Christmas tree. He studied the Nativity scene. "I wonder why we even get presents," he thought, "since it is Jesus' birthday." Carefully he picked up one of the Wise Men. The man was carrying a box of gold. "I wonder how he liked giving away his gold," Troy said to himself. Then, looking at the face of the little plastic figure, Troy noticed something he had never seen before. The Wise Man was smiling. The artist who had made the little figure had painted a holy, happy look on the Wise Man's face.

Troy was surprised. Then he remembered how the real Wise Men had traveled a great distance to give their presents to the infant Jesus. A new truth suddenly came to Troy's mind. It is not the receiving of presents that makes us so happy—it is the giving of the presents. God gave his son Jesus, and the Wise Men gave their gifts to show their love to the Savior.

Troy thought, "I still would like to keep my new toys, but I guess giving is what Christmas really is all about."

Story Questions: What had happened to the Jackson family? What did Troy want to give to the Jackson children? What figurine did Troy pick up from the Nativity scene? Was there anything unusual about the figurine? What new truth did Troy learn?

Scripture Passage: "It is more blessed to give than to receive" (Acts 20:35).

Scripture Question: How could it be more blessed to give than to receive?

Scripture Comment for Parents: In some Scripture verses the word *happy* could be used in place of the word *blessed.* This verse is saying that a great degree of happiness comes to the person who gives gifts. The giver of the gift receives no less joy from the deed than the receiver.

Prayer Suggestion: Thank God for gifts received. Ask God for opportunities to give to others.

Follow-up Activities: Prepare and take a special gift to someone who cannot give a present in return.

5
Patterns for Worship in Special Situations and Locations

Families frequently find themselves in situations, usually outside the home, which offer opportunities for unique worship experiences. Family worship related to a particular situation or location need not be as structured as planned weekly worship experiences. The situation itself will dictate the amount of time involved and the degree of structure.

This chapter includes worship resources for a variety of situation or location experiences which are common to most families. The format for this chapter is distinctively different from the previous chapter. Several action activities, stories, and Scripture passages are suggested for each situation/location experience. Any combination of suggestions from the same resource section, plus other elements the family may want to include, can be put together to create a worship experience. No attempt has been made to include food, songs, or question suggestions, but these elements could be incorporated into the worship experience if appropriate.

Family Worship While Camping

Action Activities

• Play hide-and-seek in the woods, but establish a clearly defined boundary for the playing area. Caution children about the dangers of wandering deep into the woods alone.

• Play "Camouflage." This is a modification of hide-and-seek. The person who is "It" covers his eyes until he hears no more movement on the part of the persons hiding. All the players hiding can hide as close or as far away from the "seeker" as they wish, but they must be within the sight of the "seeker" (person who is "It"). The object of the game is to use such things as bushes, leaves, branches, or rocks as camouflage with which to hide themselves. Players are not to hide completely behind any object such as a tree or a rock, but are to try to blend into the background of nature. The "seeker" never moves from the central location, but keeps turning around trying to spot the persons hiding. The last person "found" gets to be "It" for the next round.

• Use items of nature found in the camping area to make interest items which illustrate Bible stories. For example, weave twigs and vines together to make a small basket. Caulk the basket with mud and line the interior with leaves to represent the basket made for the baby Moses.

• Play "Capture the Flag." This game may require joint participation by other families at the campsite. The game would not be suitable for young preschoolers.

Divide into two teams. Each team attaches a "flag" to a tree or bush located thirty to fifty yards from the opposing flag. Establish a line at an equal distance between the two flags. The line represents the boundary between the teams' territories. The object of the game is to move into the other team's territory and capture their flag. Any player tagged while in the opponent's territory must go to the prison camp (a designated spot within the boundary of each territory). Players can "escape" from prison by being tagged by a free member of their team.

• Play "Trail Tracking." One person in the group lays a trail by using stones, bent twigs, and so forth as direction markers. All others work together to follow the trail.

• Find nature creatures. Look for bugs, insects, animals, and birds in the camp area. See how many different creatures you can locate.

• Make nature momentos. Gather leaves, blossoms, and flowers while you are camping. Use these later to make nature momentos. Place in a book for pressing. After several days of pressing and drying, use white glue to attach the items to one or more sheets of construction paper or cardboard. For an unusual effect, create a nature scene by arranging several different items on a single sheet. Display the completed work in the child's room or on the kitchen bulletin board.

Another way to preserve nature momentos is to dip the leaves and flowers into melted paraffin. Display in a vase or bowl.

• Make "cave man" inscriptions. Take partially burnt sticks from the campfire. Use the charred ends to write or draw on rocks.

• Play "Sound Track." This activity is especially suited for night, but it can be used in the daytime also. Have each family member be absolutely still for several minutes. Tell each person to try to count how many different sounds they hear. After a period of silent listening, ask each family member to try to describe the sounds he heard. Try to identify the source for each sound. Repeat the process until everyone has become sensitive to each of the sounds identified.

Stories

GIDEON BREAKS THE ENEMY CAMP

Gideon was appointed by God to lead the Israelites against the army of the Midianites. The Midianites had long oppressed the Israelites and made them poor.

Gideon called the men of Israel together to form the Israelite army. Over thirty thousand Israelite men volunteered to be in the Israelite army. They gathered on Mount Gilead.

God spoke to Gideon. "There are too many men in your army," he said. "When I give you victory over the Midianites, the men will think that they won by their own power rather than by my power."

Following God's instructions, Gideon said to his army, "If any of you are afraid to fight the Midianites, return to your homes immediately." Twenty-two thousand men left the camp and returned home. Now Gideon had only ten thousand men.

But God again told Gideon that he had too many men. God told Gideon to send the remaining men to get a drink of water. Most of the men got down on their hands and knees at the water's edge and put their faces into the water in order to drink. A few men knelt but did not put their heads down into the water. Instead, these men cupped their hands to get a little water, and then drank from the water in their hands. There were only three hundred who drank from their hands.

God then told Gideon to send everyone home except those who had drunk from their hands. Now with only three hundred men, Gideon was ready to follow God's orders and attack the huge Midianite army encamped in the valley below them.

Gideon gave each man a horn, an empty pitcher (like a vase or large jar with a wide top opening), and a torch which was placed inside the pitcher. Then he told the men what to do when he gave the signal. The brave Israelites moved out quickly to take their positions surrounding the camp of the Midianites.

When it was late at night and very dark, Gideon and one hundred men suddenly appeared outside the Midianite camp. Gideon and the men with him blew their horns. At the same time, the remaining two hundred Israelites rose from their hiding places surrounding the camp, and blew their horns. Then all the men broke their pitchers which concealed the burning torches. They held their torches high, blew their horns again, and shouted "The sword of the Lord, and of Gideon!"

The Midianites probably never really understood what happened that night. They were startled by the first blast of the horns and were surprised to realize that the sound came from around the entire camp. Then they were frightened by the strange sounds which echoed throughout the valley—the crashing sounds of breaking pottery. The sudden appearance of lights all around the camp caused them to be greatly confused. By the time they heard the second blast from the horns, and the shouts of "The sword of the Lord, and of Gideon," the Midianites were certain that a mighty army was about to descend upon their camp. Each Midianite rushed from his tent with one thought in mind—to get away before the Israelites could catch him.

God gave Gideon and his men victory over the Midianites, who never again oppressed the Israelites. Gideon learned that God would bless those who followed his instructions, even when facing a powerful enemy. He also learned that God did not always need a large number of people to achieve great things. All God needs is a few committed people.

Jacob and the Rock Pile

Jacob must have been lonely the night he looked around for stones which were smooth enough to serve as a pillow. Probably he was thinking back to the comfort of his father's tent and the joyful companionship of his mother. There would be no comfort or companionship for him that night. He had traveled a long way from home, and there was still a long journey ahead before he reached his uncle's home.

The sun had set and Jacob could not reach a village or another dwelling before nightfall. It wasn't easy to find pillow stones in the growing darkness. Setting up camp after dark, even for one person, has its problems. The chilly night air would have made anyone wish for a warm tent.

When Jacob wrapped a cover around himself and laid his head on the stone pillow, he must have again thought about the home he had just left. Any thoughts of home would have included his brother, Esau. Esau was angry with Jacob and had threatened to kill him. Jacob listened to every night sound. He was afraid that Esau had followed him and would kill him as soon as he went to sleep.

Jacob knew that Esau had every right to be angry with him. Esau was the oldest of the twins and was entitled to certain rights in the family. Once when Esau returned from a hunting trip extremely hungry, Jacob refused to share any food until Esau would give him the birthright. At another time, Jacob tricked their blind father, Isaac, into giving Jacob a special blessing which had been intended for Esau. That's when Esau became so angry that he began making plans to kill Jacob.

Esau's threats were the main reason that Jacob was not traveling to his uncle's house. Jacob hoped that if he left home for a while, Esau would forget what had happened.

When Jacob finally fell asleep, he had a dream. In his dream he saw a ladder reaching from earth to heaven and angels were going up and down the ladder. Then God appeared above the ladder and told Jacob that the land where Jacob was sleeping would someday belong to Jacob and all his children. God then promised to be with Jacob wherever he went.

Jacob awoke from his dream much more frightened than when he had gone to sleep. He said to himself, "The Lord is in this place, and I didn't know it."

Jacob used the stones that had been his pillow to mark the spot where he had the dream. He named the place Bethel, which in Hebrew means "the house of God." From that time on, Jacob trusted in God and obeyed his commandments. Jacob did not see his brother Esau again for many years, but when they did meet again, they met in peace.

FISHERMEN AND FISHERWOMEN

"That was a beautiful cast, Molly," said Grandfather as he watched the sinker on Molly's fishing line drop into the water. "You are almost as good as your mother was when she was your age."

"How do I do, Grandfather? How do I do?" asked Tim, Molly's younger brother.

"Oh you do fine also, Tim," laughed Grandfather. "I'm glad I gave you and Molly those rods and reels for Christmas. Pretty soon you both will be fishing like old-timers."

"Maybe we'll even be as good at fishing as were Peter and Andrew," said Tim.

"Don't forget James and John," said Molly. "They were fishermen too. Say, how come there weren't any fisherwomen in the Bible, Grandfather?"

"I knew that you'd ask me some question like that before the day was over, Molly," said Grandfather, with a twinkle in his eye. "In Bible times fishing was considered to be strictly a man's job—and it was a tough job."

"What was so tough about it?" asked Molly, slightly miffed. "You just said that soon Tim and I would be fishing like old-timers."

"So I did," replied Grandfather, "but Peter, Andrew, James, and John didn't fish like you do. Remember that they made their living fishing. Catching just one fish at a time would have been too slow."

"Did they put more than one hook on their line?" asked Tim.

"No," said Grandfather. "They didn't use lines at all. They used huge nets which had heavy weights and floats attached. They would throw out their nets from the side of a boat. The nets would trap the fish, and then the fishermen would pull the nets back into the boat. Even when the nets were empty it was a hard job to pull them. And when the nets were filled with fish, it took a lot of strength to get the fish on board."

"I don't think I want to do that kind of fishing," muttered Tim.

"Don't forget that Peter and the others did other kinds of fishing," said Grandfather.

"What do you mean?" asked Molly.

Grandfather sat down on a stump at the water's edge and said, "One day Peter and Andrew were in their boat near the shore on the Sea of Galilee. They were casting their net into the sea when Jesus called to them from the shore. He said to them, 'Follow me, and I will make you fishers of men.' And Peter and Andrew immediately left their boat. A little further down the shoreline they found James and John, with their father, repairing fish nets. Jesus gave the same invitation to these two brothers, and they also immediately went with Jesus."

Tim looked puzzled. "Did that mean that they went around

throwing fish nets over people's heads?"

Molly snickered, and Grandfather had a difficult time keeping a straight face. Then Grandfather smiled and said to Tim, "It does sound like that is what I meant, Tim. What Jesus meant was that the people who followed him would try to get other people to follow Jesus also. From that day on, Peter, Andrew, James, and John were much more interested in finding people who would accept Christ as their Savior than they were in finding fish in the sea."

"Say," said Molly, "there were fisherwomen in the Bible after all."

"Now I don't understand," said Grandfather.

"Why, it is easy to understand," replied Molly. "The Bible tells us about Christian women, such as Lydia and Priscilla. They were trying to lead people to Christ just like the men— so they were fisherwomen."

Grandfather raised his hands and stood up. "I give up, Molly," he said. "You're too sharp for me. Let's go cook the fish we caught.'

Scripture Verses

"And, behold, I am with thee, and will keep thee in all places whither thou goest, and will bring thee again into this land; for I will not leave thee, until I have done that which I have spoken to thee of" (Gen. 28:15).

"Surely the Lord is in this place; and I knew it not" (Gen. 28:16).

"This is none other but the house of God, and this is the gate of heaven" (Gen. 28:17).

"It is written, Man shall not live by bread alone, but by every word that proceedeth out of the mouth of God" (Matt. 4:4).

"The people which sat in darkness saw great light; and to them which sat in darkness in the region and shadow of death light is sprung up" (Matt. 4:16).

"The grass withereth, the flower fadeth: but the word of our God shall stand forever" (Isa. 40:8).

Family Worship While Traveling in a Car

Action Activities

• Play "Find-the-Alphabet." Find each letter of the alphabet, in order from *A* to *Z*, on roadside signs and auto license plates. The entire family can work as a team, or divide into two teams with each team limited to signs on one side of the road. The first team reaching *Z* is the winner.

• Play "Grandmother Went Around the World." The first player says, "Grandmother went around the world, and in her trunk she took . . ." and names an object which begins with the letter *A*. The second player repeats exactly what the first player said, but adds an object which begins with the letter *B*. Each player repeats all that has been said previously, and adds the next letter object. Continue until the alphabet is completed.

• Tell a "group story." One person begins a story and tells as much as he likes but does not complete the story. The second person must continue the story from where the first person stopped. Continue until each person has told part of the story. The last person must bring the story to a conclusion.

• Play "Pretend Hide-and-Seek." One person is designated as "It." That person pretends that he is hiding in some location within the car, such as in the glove compartment, under the seat, or in the dome light. Other persons try to guess where he is hiding. The first person to find the hiding place is "It" for the next game.

• Play "Car Count." Assign a color to each person in the car. Each person is to look for cars of his assigned color. The winner is the person with the highest number of cars found within a specific time. Change color assignments each time you play the game.

• Play "Guess Where You Are." This game is for everyone except the driver. Take turns selecting a distant landmark ahead on the highway. Then close your eyes until you think the car has reached the landmark. Before opening your eyes, call out, "Now." The driver acts as judge to determine who wins each round.

- Memorize Bible verses and review verses previously learned. Vary the review method. For example, quote the first part of a verse and let the child complete the verse. Or, call out the Scripture reference and ask the child to recite the verse.

- Play "Guess Who I Am." Each person secretly chooses a favorite Bible character, such as Moses, Paul, John the Baptist, or Peter. Take turns telling something about the secret person as if that person were speaking. Other family members try to guess which Bible character is being portrayed.

Stories

THE LOST TRAVELER

"Thank goodness we're going to stop," said Caleb. "I'm tired."

"Me, too," said his cousin, Ezra, who quickly sat down resting his back against a huge boulder. "Going to Jerusalem was a lot of fun, but it is a long way home. We've been walking all day and we still are a long way from Nazareth."

"I'll be glad when the adults have something ready to eat," said Caleb. "Let's go ask our mothers when we can eat."

"You go ask," groaned Ezra, "I'm not going to take another step until I know that my feet are pointed toward food."

Caleb laughed and hurried off to find his mother. Ezra had fallen asleep by the time he returned. "Hey, wake up, sleepyhead," said Caleb as he gently shook Ezra. "Have you seen Jesus any time today?" he asked urgently.

Ezra opened his eyes but did not move. "No," he said, "is something wrong?"

"No one can find Jesus," replied Caleb. "His mother and father have asked every family in the group. They thought he was with the group when we left Jerusalem this morning."

Caleb and Ezra forgot about being tired and hungry as they helped look for Jesus. Since they too were twelve years old they knew how frightening it would be to be lost from parents and away from home.

The next morning Caleb and Ezra watched as a tearful Mary and Joseph left the group and started traveling back to Jerusalem. They had little hope of finding Jesus in the big city.

Caleb and Ezra continued their homeward journey with their parents and the rest of the travelers. The two boys felt very sad, and this made the trip seem even longer.

Several days later Caleb was startled to hear Ezra yelling at him from down the street. Ezra was running toward him, but Caleb couldn't understand what Ezra was saying.

"They're back!" gasped Ezra breathlessly, as he leaned against the wall of Caleb's house.

"Who's back?" asked Caleb.

"Jesus," panted Ezra, "Jesus and his parents. They got back this morning, and Jesus is all right."

"What happened to him? Was he kidnapped?" Caleb inquired, excitedly.

"No," replied Ezra, "His mother and father looked all over Jerusalem for him, and they finally found him at the Temple."

"The Temple!" said a surprised Caleb, "What was he doing there?"

"You never would have guessed," replied Ezra. "All the time he was away from his parents, he was in the Temple talking with the teachers there."

"What in the world would he say to the teachers in the Temple?" inquired Caleb.

"I don't know," said Ezra, "but he must have really impressed the teachers for them to keep talking with him all those days."

"What did his parents do when they found him?" asked Caleb.

"His mother said she asked Jesus why he caused so much grief by not letting them know where he was," said Ezra, "but Jesus seemed surprised that they didn't know where to look for him. Jesus said that he must be about his Father's business."

"What did that mean?" asked Caleb.

"I don't know," said Ezra, "and neither did his parents. But Jesus came on home with them."

"Somehow I feel that Jesus is a special person," said Caleb. "He seems to know more about God than anyone I know."

"He does seem special," said Caleb. "Maybe someday he'll do something to make Nazareth a famous place. Then people will travel here to Nazareth as well as to Jerusalem."

A MAN FROM AFRICA

"Are you ready to leave, sir?" said the innkeeper to the man from Africa.

"Yes, I am," replied the man. "Would you please have my chariot made ready?"

"Immediately!" said the innkeeper, as he bowed and rushed to the stable. The man from Africa was one of the most important persons who had ever stayed at this inn. The man was from the African country of Ethiopia. The innkeeper was even more impressed with the man's job than he was with what country he was from. The chariot driver had told the innkeeper that the man had great authority under Candace, the queen of the Ethiopians. He even was in charge of the queen's treasure.

The innkeeper found the chariot driver at the stable and told him that the man from Africa was ready to leave. On his way back to the inn, the innkeeper thought about his important but unusual guest. The man from Africa was not a native of Jerusalem or any nearby cities. He had traveled a great distance to worship God. And unlike other people of great authority the innkeeper had met, this man seemed more eager to learn than he was to impress people with his authority.

The man from Africa paid the innkeeper for his services and climbed into the back of his chariot. His chariot looked like a large two-wheeled cart and was pulled by two horses. As the chariot driver urged the horses forward, the African opened a scroll and began reading aloud from the Scriptures written on the scroll. The chariot driver drove slowly so that the chariot would not bounce and make it difficult for the man to read.

Not long after the chariot left the city of Jerusalem, a man named Philip, who had been sent by God, came running up alongside the chariot. Philip heard the man from Africa reading from the book of Isaiah.

"Do you understand what you are reading?" shouted Philip.

The African didn't seem a bit surprised at Philip's sudden appearance. He shouted back over the noise of the chariot wheels, "How can I understand this unless someone guide me?" And then he invited Philip to climb up into the chariot with him.

Now the verses which the African was reading told about the suffering that Christ was to experience. The verse had been written hundreds of years before the events took place. Philip explained to the man from Africa all about Christ—about his birth, his death, and his coming to life again.

Soon they came to a pool of water. The man from Africa said to Philip, "Here is water. Is there any reason I should not be baptized?"

Philip replied, "If you believe with all your heart, you may be baptized."

The African said, "I believe that Jesus Christ is the Son of God," and he commanded the driver to stop the chariot. Then Philip and the man from Africa waded into the water, and Philip baptized the man.

Philip traveled no further with the man, but the man continued on his trip home exceedingly happy because he had accepted Christ as his Savior.

THE SHIPWRECK

"Okay, the car is packed. Everybody climb on board," shouted Dad.

Jerra and Tish ran toward the car, followed by their mother. "We can't climb 'on board,' " laughed Jerra. "This is a car, not a boat."

"It's a good thing that this is not a boat," said Tish as they pulled out of the driveway. "Jerra has enough trouble with car sickness. She'd really get sick if we were on a boat."

"Thank goodness that we have medicine to prevent the car sickness," said Mother. "You did take your medicine before we left didn't you, Jerra?"

"Oh," replied Jerra, "I forgot."

"Ohhh," groaned everyone else in the car. Dad turned the car around and drove into the driveway again.

When Jerra returned to the car after taking her medicine, she said, "If we had been in a boat, it wouldn't have been so easy to have gone back for the medicine." She was trying to say something to make her family forget that she had delayed the beginning of their trip.

Jerra's father was anxious that everyone start the trip in a happy mood, so he said, "You are right, Jerra. It would not have been so easy to turn around in a boat, especially if you lived in Bible times and were traveling with the apostle Paul. Would you like to hear about his boat trip?"

"Oh, yes, tell us," exclaimed Jerra, who was glad no longer to be the center of attention.

"Was it an exciting trip?" asked Tish.

"Very exciting!" replied her father. "Almost any boat trip with Paul would have been exciting. He already had been in three shipwrecks by the time he took the trip I'll tell you about."

Both girls settled back into their seats as their father began the story.

"On this trip," said their father, "Paul was traveling from Jerusalem to Rome, which was a long distance. Paul was not on vacation. He was being sent to Rome as a prisoner because of his preaching about Christ. Roman soldiers were traveling with him to guard him. However, the commander of the soldiers, whose name was Julius, had much respect for Paul. Often Julius would ask Paul's advice about the best way to travel. Julius knew that Paul was an experienced traveler and that he would give good advice. But one time Julius did not take Paul's advice. Paul warned Julius that they should not sail from the harbor where they had spent several days. Paul said that a terrible storm would wreck the ship. But the shipmaster told Julius that the sea was calm and no storm clouds were visible, so Julius ordered the ship to sail.

They had not been sailing long until a sudden storm came up, and the ship was tossed about. On the third day of the storm the sailors threw some of the equipment overboard to lighten the ship and make it easier to handle. But still the ship was out of control. No one felt like eating because the sea was so rough.

One day while the storm was still raging, Paul stood in the midst of all the people on the ship and told them that an angel from God had spoken to him. He said that the angel assured him that no lives would be lost, even though the ship would be wrecked. So Paul urged everyone to "be of good cheer."

"How could anyone be of good cheer in a situation like that?" moaned Jerra, who was beginning to look a little pale.

"Go on, Daddy," said Tish, "What happened next?"

Dad glanced back at Jerra and decided that he had better end the story quickly without giving too many details. "The storm continued for fourteen days," he said. "Finally, early one morning before sunup, Paul urged everyone to eat some food so that they would feel better. He again reminded them of God's promise that no one would be injured. When daylight came, all the cargo was thrown overboard to make the ship even lighter. Then the sailors ran the ship straight into the shore. The front of the ship held fast, but the back part broke into pieces. Everyone quickly jumped overboard. Those who couldn't swim floated ashore on boards. Just as Paul had said, God took care of them, and no life was lost in the shipwreck."

"Paul was a brave man, wasn't he Daddy?" said Tish.

"Yes, but more important than being brave, he trusted in God," said Dad. "Anyone can be as brave as Paul if they trust God with all their heart."

Scripture Verses

"And it came to pass, that after three days they found him in the temple, sitting in the midst of the doctors, both hearing them, and asking them questions. And all that heard him were astonished at his understanding and answers" (Luke 2:46-47).

"And as they went on their way, they came unto a certain water: and the eunuch said, See, here is water; what doth hinder me to be baptized? And Philip said, If thou believest with all thine heart, thou mayest. And he answered and said, I believe that Jesus Christ is the Son of God" (Acts 8:36-37).

"And when he had thus spoken, he took bread, and gave thanks to God in presence of them all: and when he had broken it, he began to eat. Then were they all of good cheer" (Acts 27:35-36).

"Thy word is a lamp unto my feet, and a light unto my path" (Ps. 119:105).

"How beautiful upon the mountains are the feet of him that bringeth good tidings, that publisheth peace; that bringeth good tidings of good, that publisheth salvation; that saith unto Zion, Thy God reigneth!" (Isa. 52:7).

"Walk in all the ways which the Lord your God hath commanded you" (Deut. 5:33).

"Teach me thy way, O Lord" (Ps. 27:11).

Family Worship While on a Picnic

Action Activities

Most of the activities suggested for use on a camping trip would be appropriate for picnics also. In addition, picnics offer opportunities to use commercially produced outdoor games. Depending upon the age of the children, picnic activities could include volleyball, croquet, lawn bowling, badminton, soccer, horseshoes, softball, dodge ball, kickball, and football. Where the picnic is part of a swimming outing, water games should be included in the many possible choices.

Stories

DINNER ON THE GROUND

The Israelites were not happy, even though they should have been. Moses had just led them out of Egypt where they had been slaves. Their parents and grandparents before them had been slaves in Egypt for hundreds of years. But now the Egyptians no longer had control over them. Moses, following God's instructions, had led them to escape from Egypt.

Instead of always being grateful to God and to Moses, the Israelites complained bitterly every time they had difficulty. Each time a problem arose the people spoke against Moses. They said, "We would have been better off if we had stayed in Egypt as slaves." They really would not have been better off in Egypt, but they thought that anyplace would be better than where they were.

After leaving Egypt, the Israelites spent years moving from place to place in the wilderness where the land was bare and dry. Once, while they were traveling in an area called the wilderness of Shur, they traveled for three days without finding any water. Finally, they found some water, but it was so bitter that they could not stand the taste.

When the people found that the water was unfit to drink, they complained to Moses. Moses didn't know what to do, so he prayed earnestly to God for help. God showed Moses a certain tree to cut down and throw into the bitter water. After the tree was thrown into the water, the water no longer was bitter. The people then had plenty of good water to drink.

Later Moses led the Israelites to another wilderness area where they ran short of food. Again the Israelites complained to Moses, saying that they would have been better off to have died in Egypt than to die of hunger in the wilderness. They quickly forgot how God had taken care of them in the past.

God then told Moses he would provide them with plenty of bread and meat to eat. God told Moses to tell the people to take only the amount of bread they would eat on that day, no more. The only exception was to be on the day before the sabbath when they were to take enough bread to last two days.

That evening small birds called quail covered the entire camp. God had provided the Israelites meat to eat. The next morning the people found the ground covered with small white puffs which they called manna. Moses told them that the manna was the bread which God had promised. The manna had the taste of a wafer made with honey.

Moses reminded them that they were to gather only enough manna for their family to eat that day. After the people had gathered their share the hot sun melted all the manna which had been left on the ground.

Contrary to Moses' instructions, some of the people tried to save some of their manna until the next day. The next morning they found that the manna was not fit to eat. Moses was very angry with those who had not followed his instructions.

On the day before the sabbath, the people gathered enough manna to last for two days. This time the food which they kept overnight did not spoil. Moses told the people to eat that food on the sabbath because God would not provide food for them to gather on the sabbath day.

Some of the people went out on the sabbath intending to gather manna that day, but they found none on the ground. This was God's way of reminding them that they were to keep the sabbath day holy. They were to do no work that day.

God provided the people of Israel with manna each day, except the sabbath, for the entire forty years they spent wandering in the wilderness. The people knew each day that God was taking care of them.

A MEAL TO REMEMBER

"Please pass the potato salad," said Stuart.

"That's your third helping," said his mother as she handed him a bowl. "Please don't overeat. You don't want this picnic to become a bad memory."

"No, I don't" replied Stuart, "but what you said just now

reminds me of something I have been meaning to ask for a long time."

"What's your question?" his father asked.

"At church there is a table in front of the pulpit, and carved into the table are the words "In Remembrance of Me." I know that the table is used when the Lord's Supper is served, but I don't understand the purpose of the table or of the Lord's Supper. Why do you eat and drink in a worship service?"

Stuart's father rested his elbows on the picnic table while he thought about the question. Then he said, "Stuart, I hadn't realized it until you asked that question, but eating a special meal was an important part of worship in both Old Testament times before Christ, and in New Testament times after Christ came."

"Why was it important?" inquired Stuart.

"In both the Old Testament and the New Testament, the meal served as a reminder of the great things God had done for the people who believed in him. Just before God led the people of Israel out of Egypt where they had been slaves for over four hundred years, he told them to eat a special meal called the Passover. It was given that name because on that night the death angel took the life of the firstborn in every house except the houses of the Israelites. The death angel passed over the Israelite houses. God knew that after the death angel struck, the king of Egypt would tell the Israelites to leave the country. Therefore God instructed that the Passover meal was to be eaten quickly—so quickly that the people were not even to wait for the bread dough to puff up before they baked it. Then God told the Israelites that they should eat the Passover meal at the same time each year as a reminder of how God freed them from slavery.

"What about the Lord's Supper?" asked Stuart. "How did it get started?"

"The Lord's Supper," said his father, "was begun by Jesus, but the first Lord's Supper was part of a Passover meal."

"How did that happen?" inquired Stuart.

"The Bible tells us that Jesus gave his disciples instructions
on how to prepare for the Passover meal," Stuart's father said.
"Then all the disciples met for the meal in an upstairs room."

Stuart's father took a small New Testament from his pocket,
opened it, and handed it to Stuart saying, "Here, read aloud
what happened next. Read these two verses."

Stuart read, "And he took bread, and gave thanks, and brake
it, and gave unto them, saying, This is my body which is given
for you: this do in remembrance of me. Likewise also the cup
after supper, saying, This cup is the new testament in my blood,
which is shed for you" (Luke 22:19-20).

"Now I understand," said Stuart. "The Lord's Supper is a
reminder of what Christ did for us. That is why the table in
front of the pulpit has the words "In Remembrance of Me."

"Now you do understand," said his father.

MOTHER'S NEW NAME

"This looks like a good spot," said Mrs. Montgomery, "but
there is no picnic table here. We'll have to spread the tablecloth
on the ground."

"That means we will have to eat quickly," said Mr. Montgomery, "because the ants will soon learn that they are on the
wrong side of the tablecloth."

Turning to the three children, Mrs. Montgomery said,
"Marge, Alex, Lewis, you may go play for a few minutes until
we get the food ready. But Marge, watch Lewis and make
sure that he doesn't wander off."

"OK, Mother," said Marge, as she led her younger brother
off to play.

In a short while Mr. Montgomery shouted, "Come on, children! Let's eat."

The children came running. After they thanked God for the
food, the hungry youngsters eagerly began calling for their
favorite foods to be passed to them. Mrs. Montgomery spooned
out the requested foods to each plate, and then she poured
everyone's drinks. By the time she had filled all the plates,

the first one served began asking for second helpings. And then all the drink cups needed to be filled again.

Finally Mr. Montgomery said to his wife, "You're spending all your time serving us. Let us take care of ourselves while you eat."

"Oh, you'll just have to call me 'Martha,'" said Mrs. Montgomery. "I'm more concerned that everyone get all they want."

"Why should we call you 'Martha'?" asked Alex. "That is not your name."

"I was just joking," replied Mrs. Montgomery. "Martha was a lady mentioned in the Bible who was overly concerned about preparing a meal. Jesus had come to her house to visit. While Martha spent a great deal of time in the kitchen preparing food, her younger sister, Mary, just sat and listened to Jesus talk. Finally Martha became so upset because her sister wasn't helping that she complained to Jesus about it. She asked Jesus if he really didn't care that Mary had left her alone to do all the work."

"Didn't Jesus care?" asked Marge.

"Oh yes," replied Mrs. Montgomery, "but Jesus said that the younger sister had chosen to do the best thing—and that was to learn more about God."

"Then we should call you Mary Martha, Mother," said Alex, "because you read the Bible to learn more about God, and you also spend a lot of time preparing food for us."

The rest of the family laughed and agreed that Mrs. Montgomery should have a new name.

Scripture Verses

"The Lord is my strength and song, and he is become my salvation" (Ex. 15:2).

"And Moses said unto them, This is the bread which the Lord had given you to eat" (Ex. 16:15).

"The Lord Jesus the same night in which he was betrayed took bread: And when he had given thanks, he brake it, and said, Take, eat: this is my body, which is broken for you: this do in remembrance of me" (1 Cor. 11:23-24).

"For as often as ye eat this bread, and drink this cup, ye do shew the Lord's death till he come" (1 Cor. 11:26).

"Therefore take no thought, saying, What shall we eat? or, What shall we drink? or, Wherewithal shall we be clothed? . . . for your heavenly Father knoweth that ye have need of all these things" (Matt. 6:31).

Family Worship While Waiting

Families frequently spend time waiting for someone. Usually the waiting is for one of the parents. The family may sit in the car while the mother shops at the grocery or runs an errand. Or, they may be waiting for the father to get off from work or until his plane lands at the airport. Family waiting takes place at churches, schools, bus and airline terminals, hospital lobbies, hotel lobbies, doctor's offices, parking lots, and service stations. Often the waiting time could become another worship opportunity.

Unless you carry a copy of this book in your car, perhaps the best way to utilize the following resources is to plan ahead. Choose one or two of the action activities and become familiar with the suggested procedures. Then select one story and study it enough to remember the basic outline. It is not necessary to memorize a story word for word. Finally, choose one of the suggested Scripture verses and memorize it. Now you are prepared for the next waiting experience. Since children enjoy repetition, plan to use the selected resources at least twice before preparing a new "program" for a waiting worship experience.

Action Activities

• Play "Riddle Riddle Marie." This old favorite was suggested for one of the weekly experiences, but it is especially suited for waiting situations where the activity must be more mental than physical. One person says "Riddle Riddle Marie, I see something that you don't see, and the color of it is . . ."

The first person who guesses the object gets to select the next object.

- Play "Clap-a-Song." Choose a simple song or nursery rhyme that has a distinctive beat. Everyone sings the song together, but claps the beat at the same time. Repeat the song but leave off the last word. Clap the beat instead. Continue repeating the song, but drop off an additional word each time. Continue until you clap through the entire song without singing a word.

- Make up stories about people you see while waiting. Guess what type of work you think they might do, give them a fictitious name, and create a make-believe story about them. Take turns choosing people and telling stories.

- Play a counting game. For example, count how many people you see who wear brown shoes, or open a door with their left hand, or wear some type of head covering.

- If pencil and paper are available, let each person draw various objects, people, or scenes which can be seen from your waiting location.

- Use the waiting time to review meaningful verses of Scripture, or to learn the books of the Bible.

Stories

WAITING IN ANGER

Mr. Martin walked briskly across the air terminal lobby to rejoin his family.

"When is Uncle Bob's plane coming in?" yelled Brad, as soon as he saw his father approaching.

"Not so loud!" cautioned his mother. "Your father will tell you as soon as he gets here."

"But I want to know now!" declared Brad, impatiently. "We've been waiting a long time for Uncle Bob."

"I'm afraid that we'll have to wait a little longer," said Mr. Martin, as he sat down with his family. "Uncle Bob's plane has been delayed another thirty minutes because of the weather. And you, young man," he said, pointing at Brad, "will have to control your temper. There is no need for you to be so angry."

Brad slid down in his seat meekly and said, "I'm sorry, but we have been waiting a long time, and nothing has happened."

"Suppose I tell you a story about a man who became angry because nothing happened after he waited and waited," said Brad's father.

"Neat," said Brad. "Is the man someone I know?"

"Not exactly," replied Mr. Martin, "but you may have heard about him at church. His name was Jonah."

"Is that the same man who was swallowed by a big fish?" asked Brad.

"Yes, it is," said his father.

"But I didn't know that he was angry," said Brad.

"Then let me tell you the entire story," said Mr. Martin. "God told Jonah to go to a certain large city and preach to the people there. The people of that city were very wicked. But instead of going to the city, Jonah tried to get away from God by taking a ship headed in a different direction."

"That's when Jonah wound up inside a huge fish, wasn't it?" said Brad.

"Yes," said Mr. Martin, "God caused a storm which tossed the ship around. When the sailors found out that Jonah was the reason for the storm, they threw him overboard. Then the large fish which God had prepared swallowed Jonah. After Jonah had spent three days in the fish's stomach, Jonah was ready to obey God and go preach in the large city."

"Is that when Jonah became angry?" asked Brad.

"No, it wasn't," said Mr. Martin. "Jonah went to the city and preached that God would destroy the city because of the wickedness of the people. When the people of the city heard what Jonah preached, they became very sorry for what they had done. And when God saw how sorry all the people were, he decided not to destroy the city. That is what made Jonah so angry. He had gone outside the city and had waited a long time to see it destroyed. He waited and waited, but nothing

happened. He was angry because the destruction he had pre-
dicted did not take place."

"You mean he cared more about being right than about an
entire city of people?" asked Brad.

"It reminds me of someone who was more concerned about
being bored while waiting than about his uncle having a safe
trip," said Mr. Martin.

"Oh, I see what you mean," said Brad, "I guess God does
want us to care about other people."

"Doesn't anyone care about saying 'hello' to me?" said Uncle
Bob who had walked up unnoticed.

"I do!" shouted Brad, and he gave his uncle a big hug.

WAITING IN FEAR

"I'm frightened, Daddy," said Faye as she snuggled closer
to her father. "Sitting here in the car while it is raining, thun-
dering, and lightning is no fun. Why can't Mommy come on?
It shouldn't take so long to get the groceries."

"Your mother will be here just as soon as she can, Faye,"
said her father. "There are a lot of people shopping today. I
imagine that she will have to wait in line for a little while
even when she has loaded her shopping cart."

"Just the same," replied Faye, "I do wish she would hurry.
It's raining so hard that I can't see much through the car windows. It makes me feel like we are here all alone. And that
thunder and lightning is scary. It's like we were trapped by
the storm in a cave."

"I hadn't thought of it that way before," said her father.
"The car does resemble a cave, and being here reminds me
of an Old Testament prophet who was in a cave during a
storm."

"Tell me about it," said Faye. "Maybe it will help me not
be so scared—or at least maybe it will make the time go faster."

"The prophet's name," began her father, "was Elijah, and
he knew what it was like to be scared. The king's wife, Jezebel,
was angry with Elijah because he had proved that the prophets

she supported were false prophets. Being a false prophet meant that they preached about a god who didn't exist. Elijah had called all the false prophets together. He asked them to show that the god they preached about was real. When the false prophets couldn't do what Elijah asked, Elijah proved to them that God of the Israelites was real.

"Instead of being glad to know about the real God, Jezebel was angry with Elijah. She sent word to Elijah that she would have him killed by the next day. Elijah was very frightened because he knew that Jezebel was mean enough to do exactly what she said.

"Elijah decided that the only way he could stay alive was to get as far away from Jezebel as he could. He traveled for forty days until he found a cave where he could hide. The cave was in the side of a mountain."

"Was the cave as big as our car?" asked Faye.

"It probably was bigger," continued her father, "but while he was there, a strong wind blew across the mountain. It blew so hard that rocks were broken. Then after the wind came an earthquake, and then fire came down upon the mountain. All the while Elijah was waiting for God to speak to him, but God did not speak to him through the wind, or the earthquake, or the fire."

"How did God speak?" asked Faye.

"The Bible says," explained her father, "that after the fire there was a 'still small voice,' and that was God."

"Was he afraid of God?" Faye asked eagerly.

"No," her father replied. "One reason that Elijah was so afraid was because he thought that he was the only person left on earth who worshiped the true God. God showed him that there were at least seven thousand other believers in Israel. From that time on, Elijah knew that God would protect him from the wicked queen."

"I'm glad that God gives us other people to be with us when we are afraid, aren't you, Daddy?" said Faye.

"Yes, I am," said her father as he kissed her forehead.

WAITING IN FAITH

Jo Lynn and her mother were sitting on a stone bench next to the water fountain at a large, enclosed shopping center. Jo Lynn's father and older brother had gone to an automobile supply store in the shopping center. Shortly after Jo Lynn's father and brother had left, a woman wearing lots of heavy makeup got a drink and then sat down on the bench next to Jo Lynn's mother. Jo Lynn did not like the looks of the woman at all. The woman seemed like she might have been the same age as Jo Lynn's mother, but the hardness of her face and her rough speech made the woman seem older. What displeased Jo Lynn the most was that the woman tried to dress like she was much younger. And her obviously dyed hair was styled just like that of the teenagers at church.

Jo Lynn at first did not pay too much attention to her mother's conversation with the woman. Sometimes the woman used bad words, and Jo Lynn knew that her mother would not want her to listen.

After a while Jo Lynn realized that the woman, who at first had been loud and boisterous, was doing less and less talking. The woman seemed very interested in what Jo Lynn's mother was saying. Jo Lynn was shocked into full attention when she realized that her mother was telling the woman a Bible story.

Jo Lynn's mother was telling about the time Jesus' disciples had gone into a town to buy food, but Jesus had decided to wait for them at a certain well. While Jesus was sitting on the well resting, a woman from the town came with empty water jugs. Jesus surprised the woman by asking her for a drink from one of her jugs. The woman was surprised that Jesus spoke to her for two reasons. First, Jesus was a Jew, and Jews usually had nothing to do with Samaritans such as she. Another reason for her surprise was that she did not have a good reputation in the town. Most of the respectable people would avoid any contact with her. The woman at the well was even more surprised when Jesus told her things about her life that she thought were secret. The woman finally realized that Jesus was the Christ, and then she brought other people to meet him.

After her mother finished telling the story, Jo Lynn saw that the woman sitting on the bench had tears in her eyes. The woman took Jo Lynn's mother's hand and held it tightly for a few moments. Then the woman thanked Jo Lynn's mother for giving her something more valuable than anything she had bought that day.

Jo Lynn didn't understand it, but somehow the woman looked much nicer when she left than she did when she first sat down by the water fountain.

Scripture Verses

"When my soul fainted within me I remembered the Lord: and my prayer came in unto thee, into thine holy temple" (Jonah 2:7).

"And, behold, the Lord passed by, and a great and strong wind rent the mountains, and broke in pieces the rocks before the Lord; but the Lord was not in the wind: and after the wind an earthquake; but the Lord was not in the earthquake: And after the earthquake a fire; but the Lord was not in the fire: and after the fire a still small voice" (1 Kings 19:11-12).

"But whosoever drinketh of the water that I shall give him shall never thirst; but the water that I shall give him shall be in him a well of water springing up into everlasting life" (John 4:14).

"But the hour cometh, and now is, when the true worshipers shall worship the Father in spirit and in truth: for the Father seeketh such to worship him" (John 4:23).

"God is a Spirit: and they that worship him must worship him in spirit and in truth" (John 4:24).

"Now we believe, not because of thy sayings: for we have heard him ourselves, and know that this is indeed the Christ, the Saviour of the world" (John 4:42).

Topical Listing
of Story Titles